AINSLIE ON JOCKEYS/The Relationship of Jockeys to the Winning and Losing of Horse Races

by Tom Ainslie

SIMON AND SCHUSTER / NEW YORK

Designed by Irving Perkins
Manufactured in the United States of America

2   3   4   5   6   7   8   9   10   11

Library of Congress Cataloging in Publication Data

Ainslie, Tom.
    Ainslie on jockeys.

    First ed. published in 1967 under title: Ainslie's jockey book.
    1. Jockeys.   2. Horse-racing.   I. Title.
SF334.A5   1975   798′.4   75–6991

Contents

Preface to the Second Edition

MUCH HAS CHANGED DURING THE EIGHT YEARS SINCE THE FIRST edition of this book was published. Many leading race riders and trainers of the late 1960's are no longer around. And some of today's stars were unknown then. The book needs alteration on those grounds alone.

Moreover, handicapping—the game of trying to predict the outcome of races—is no longer what it was. Science has overtaken us. A scholar named Frederick S. Davis has published the first competent study of performance statistics in the history of the sport. (*Thoroughbred Racing: Percentages and Probabilities,* Millwood, N.Y., 10546: Millwood Publications, 1974). His work fortifies the selection process with an objectivity and dependability often lacking in the theories and procedures of less-scientific handicappers. I include myself but do not apologize. On the contrary, I am pleased that some of my favorite notions (so laboriously developed through trial and error) have been verified by the Davis statistics. And I welcome the chance to enlarge my arsenal with new weapons.

Accordingly, the comprehensively detailed handicapping method set forth in the first edition of this book has now been embellished and upgraded.

It was pretty effective before the improvements. Dozens of readers have assured me that they have been making good livings with it.

Could be. But only a special personality can long endure the daily anxiety of trying to make a living by betting on horses. For the rest of us, handicapping is best approached as a game. A great game.

TOM AINSLIE

New York
1975

Bets . . . fool-traps, where the wise, like spiders, lay in ambush for the flies.

—JOHN DRYDEN

If thou desire to raise thy fortunes, be wise. . . . It is a bad voyage where the pilot is blind.

—FRANCIS QUARLES

ONE / *Why Horseplayers Die Bald*

A GENIAL HUSTLER WHO EARNS HIS $250 SUITS, HIS MANICURES, and the other necessities of his life by running discreet errands for various horsemen, ambled up to my companion and me at Aqueduct one afternoon a while ago. From the side of his mouth came a quiet revelation.

"We're going today," he murmured. "He figures real big. We're getting down heavy and look for an honest two to one."

Translation: A stable, which employed this man, was confident that one of its horses would win a race that afternoon. The stable was betting a considerable amount of money and anticipated a pari-mutuel payoff of at least $6.

Anyone capable of reading and analyzing the past-performance records in the *Daily Racing Form* did not need this inside information. The horse's chart stood out on the printed page like a ruby stickpin. It won its race in a canter. But it only paid even money. Winners as clearly predictable as this seldom pay decent prices at Aqueduct. The New York racing crowd is the shrewdest in the United States.

However, a racing audience can be the shrewdest in the United States and still be awfully dumb. In another race that day several tip sheets and a majority of the newspaper selectors favored an animal whose record justified no such optimism. The horse, a front-

11

runner, was entered at an uncomfortable distance against other front-runners who figured to cook its goose with a fast early pace. While watching the totalisator board and marveling at the zeal with which the crowd was driving down the odds on this misplaced creature, I learned on unimpeachable authority that the horse's owner and trainer were betting a bundle. Did they know something? Was it possible that the elementary principles of horse-race handicapping were not applicable to this race? Yes, it was possible. It is always possible. Any race can be won by any horse, racing luck being what it is.

The animal went to the post a 6 to 5 favorite, was run into the ground by a fast pace during the first half-mile, and finished out of the money. The principles of handicapping had not been suspended. The horse did not figure to win, and it did not win.

My purpose in offering these two anecdotes is to suggest that the horseplayer who takes the trouble to master the intricacies of the past-performance records and become a good handicapper has the best possible chance to beat the races. He very likely will become a better handicapper than the average horseman. In any case, he will be immeasurably better off than the poor soul who relies on inside information, much of which is worthless. To strengthen the argument, let me point out that it is not at all unusual for as many as five horses to have predictably good chances to win a particular race. In such a case, it also is not unusual for the owners, trainers, and hangers-on at two or three of the five barns to wager hundreds—perhaps thousands—of dollars. They can't all be right. A horseplayer acting on inside information from one of the betting stables involved in a lottery of that kind is in a far less secure position than is the expert handicapper, who ignores such information. The expert handicapper knows, for instance, that the race is too close and should not be played.

As readers of *The Compleat Horseplayer* (New York: Simon & Schuster, 1966) understand, sound handicapping requires a working knowledge of the following interrelated subjects: distance, form, weight, class, sex, consistency, jockey, pace, the horse's appearance and behavior in the paddock, and a few dozen Plus Factors deriving from the stable's manipulations, the horse's current form cycle, and other crucial matters. All but a small fraction of such information is available in the *Daily Racing Form*. The rest is obtained from *The American Racing Manual*, the track's daily printed program, and from personal observation of horses in the saddling enclosure.

Among the numerous mysteries of handicapping that have to be solved—or at least partly solved—before the player can hope to prosper at the track, none is more mysterious than the relationship of the jockey to the outcome of the race. It is possible to set forth rules (as I have in various books) that (a) prevent the player from betting a horse whose chances are worsened by the trainer's choice of jockey, and (b) direct the player's favor toward the horse whose rider is likely to fit the assignment. But rules are not nearly as useful as the fundamental knowledge from which rules are made.

In the following pages, the reader will find a great deal about race riding as an art and a profession. The purpose is *not* to add yet another nostalgic volume to the colorful lore of the turf. The purpose is to help the reader pick more winners and avoid more losers.

Therefore, we have here an entirely new kind of handicapping manual, designed to help the player understand, at long last, how the trainer's choice of jockey relates to all other aspects of handicapping. In the process of acquiring this understanding, the player will undoubtedly find himself brushing up on fundamental handicapping principles. Like as not, he will also absorb a number of the finer points of the pastime. And the day will come when he will leave the track with more money in his wallet than he had when he arrived. And the time may also come when he can consult his ledger and say, "What do you know? I'm ahead on the year!"

An experience so glorious never befalls the player of "systems." An example: Every follower of the game knows that, in any given month, certain jockeys are "hot" (winning rather more frequently than usual) and others are "cold" (losing rather more frequently than usual). Incredible numbers of players transform this superficial knowledge into a creed, a "system." They bet on jockeys, without regard for the records of the horses. Financially speaking, these gamblers get their heads handed to them. They all lose in the long run, and many of them lose in the short run as well. The reasons are not hard to come by: Even the greatest and most fortunate of jockeys seldom wins more than once in every five starts. Furthermore, this low average is achieved by running hot and cold. I can think of no leading rider who has not encountered streaks of twenty, thirty, and even fifty successive losses.

Anyone who hopes to survive at the track must do better than that. The good handicapper therefore looks for a race in which one horse not only has an excellent chance to win but is under a jockey who— regardless of reputation—figures to be more than equal to the specific demands of the occasion. The good handicapper's bet is a speculation—a guess—but of the very smartest sort. It is an informed guess. It is a guess fortified by reasoned analysis of all available facts. A good handicapper can expect to guess correctly from one-third to one-half of the time. If he seldom speculates on favorites, his percentage of winners will be at the lower end of that scale. If he accepts horses at low odds, he will cash as many as half of his tickets. In either case, he will show a profit at the end of the year, and even the month, and often the week.

To give the reader some notion of the complexities of the relationship between jockeys and the winning or losing of races, let me tell a story about Braulio Baeza, one of the best riders in the United States. Until 1965, supremacy was generally conceded to Willie Shoemaker. But during that year Baeza, a laconic Panamanian, won more often (270 races) than Shoe and accounted for $2,582,702 in purse money. This was almost as much as Shoemaker had won in his best years.

"And it was harder dough to win," confides one of the sages of the Aqueduct clubhouse. "Baeza was riding in New York. The competition here is the toughest in the country. Shoemaker does most of his best work in California, where he practically owns the tracks and has everything his way. When Shoemaker tries to crack New York he's just another boy. Goes for days without a winner."

Baeza is one of the best. So is Shoemaker. But ever since 1970 the top accolade has been reserved for Laffit Pincay, Jr., another Panamanian but fantastic. He led all riders in terms of purses won during that year and each of the next four. In 1973 all Pincay did was win 24.2 percent of his 1,444 starts—350 victories for an all-time record of $4,093,492 in purse earnings. The previous record, just under $3.8 million, was set by Pincay in 1971. Unlike Shoemaker, an all-time great who sometimes had trouble handling large, stubborn, heavy-headed horses like Kelso and Native Dancer, Pincay seems able to win on anything. And he customarily leads every meeting in which he competes, whether in California or New York.

One would expect that the presence of a top-notch rider on a first-class horse would make it a fantastically good bet against second-rate competition. Such expectations were rampant at Aqueduct on May 18, 1966, when Baeza went to the post aboard Bold Lad for the twenty-fourth running of the Roseben Handicap, a seven-furlong sprint. Bold Lad had been everybody's early choice in the 1965 Kentucky Derby, but he had been hobbled by leg injuries and had finished tenth. After a full year of rest the beautiful Wheatley Stable chestnut had come back to the races and quickly established himself as the best-looking sprinter in the East.

So the crowd made him an odds-on favorite in the Roseben.

He should have won in a walk.

I watched the race on closed-circuit television with a bunch of jockeys' agents and trainers in their lair under the clubhouse.

"He's in a switch!" cried an agent happily as the horses streaked down the homestretch. "They got him in a pocket!"

Baeza had been keeping the horse under a steady hold all the way, laying fourth, saving ground by running close to the rail. But now the move, the finishing kick, was due, and Baeza had no place to go. He was behind a wall of horses. And they were running fast. If

Baeza tried to go outside to find racing room, he would lose too much ground, too much time, and the race.

As we contemplated this possibility, Johnny Rotz's tiring mount, Beaupy, began to drift out slightly. The instant this happened, Bold Lad flowed through the opening like air into a vacuum. There did not seem to be enough room between Beaupy and Manuel Ycaza's Hoist Bar for a horse to get through, but Bold Lad penetrated without bumping anyone. It was a magnificent display of winning spirit by the colt. It was an incredible display of guts and alertness by the jockey. Bold Lad won going away.

"Did you ever see anything like that?" said one of the jockey agents.

"Nuts!" or a word to that effect, retorted another. "That's Bold Lad. If I was riding Bold Lad the same thing would of happened. Just let Baeza ride some of the cripples I gotta ride."

Agents refer to their jockeys as "I." A barnacle on the keel of the *Queen Elizabeth 2* which announced, "I set a new transatlantic record last week," would sound less pretentious than a jockey agent telling his cronies about how "I" ride winners.

Be that as it may, the Roseben was an exciting race.

Why do horseplayers die bald? Because they tear their hair out. If Beaupy had been a bit more horse and had not given way, Bold Lad would have lost the race. Whereupon a legion of exasperated, freshly impoverished chalk players would have been entitled to ask some searching questions. What was Baeza doing in that pocket in the first place? How come he hadn't moved to the outside on the turn for home? What made him think the other horse would bear out and give him room?

Horseplayers—especially the players of losing favorites—frequently ask such questions. Loudly. They never get answers. On this occasion, of course, they had no questions to ask. Bold Lad had won, which made good handicappers of them all. They were too pleased with themselves to harbor the idea that they had been the beneficiaries of extreme good luck.

16

Braulio Baeza's face looks like hand-carved mahogany. "I was behind horses with no place to go, just waiting for an opening," he said, adding that when the opening occurred his mount had taken good advantage of it. He did not explain *why* he had been behind horses with no place to go, especially since he had the fastest and classiest animal in the race and could have won as he pleased had he moved outside on the turn into the stretch.

Quite possibly, Baeza had suffered a lapse in judgment. Give him a bad mark. But now give him a good mark for courage far beyond the call of normal duty.

"How many riders do you think would have gone through that hole?" someone asked Bold Lad's trainer, Eddie Neloy.

Neloy grinned. "You mean how many *rich* riders would have gone through that hole," he answered, knowing that the answer was "not many."

So Baeza, who is rich, almost lost the race, but pulled it out of the fire with a display of reinsmanship that few other riders would have dared attempt.

The incident suggests that jockeys have more than a little to do with the winning or losing of horse races. It also shows that even a great jockey may err, and that only his greatness—and the abilities of his horse—can repair such error.

Another story provides a different kind of insight. A few years ago a betting stable had prepared one of its cheap horses for what it fondly believed would be a killing. For several races the horse was entered at the wrong distance, or at unfavorable weights, or against opponents able to set an unfavorably fast early pace. The horse's recent record looked awful. But the animal was in its best possible condition. So the trainer dropped it into a race in which everything seemed made to order. The riding assignment was given to an experienced journeyman who knew the ways of the horse. The trainer and owner bet their shirts. The tote board proclaimed something like 12 to 1 on the horse as it left the paddock for the parade to the post.

17

The owner and trainer repaired to their box, rubbing their hands happily.

"How much did you bet for the boy?" asked the owner.

"What?" asked the confident trainer.

"The boy. How many tickets did you buy him?"

"Ohmigod," moaned the trainer. "I forgot to bet anything for him."

"Well, did you at least tell him you would?"

"I forgot."

The owner turned green. "It's too late now. The little sonofabitch must think it's just another workout today."

The horse finished fifth. It came out of the gate slowly, made up a good deal of ground on the backstretch, but kept running into the rear ends of other horses.

The owner and trainer assumed that if the jockey had known that a hundred dollars were being bet for him, he would have understood that the horse was supposed to have a chance to win. They assumed that he would have hustled the animal out of the starting gate on time and would have taken pains to find adequate running room all the way. They assumed that he would have won.

They might have been right. The horse might have won. In any event, it undoubtedly would have been navigated differently.

Does this mean that the jockey deliberately threw the race? Not at all. But it does mean that there is more to some races than the innocent eye can recognize. Journeymen jocks below the first rank rely for their living on winning cheap races. Many of the stables that enter such races seek extra revenue through the kind of manipulation that produces winners at good mutuel prices. The journeyman jockey knows better than to overexert a cheap horse on a day when it has no real chance to win. To do so may empty the beast of the spirit and energy it will need on a later, more favorable occasion.

How, then, does the boy know that today is the day for all-out effort? One of the most eloquently persuasive methods trainers and owners have found for communicating this intelligence to some jockeys is by betting for them and telling them so. Indeed, as the anecdote illustrates, betting stables cannot hope to get a winning ride from certain jocks unless the bet is made.

It should be emphasized that this sort of thing is a considerable distance from the actual rigging of races. That form of larceny used to be widespread but seems now to occur only at lesser tracks, supervision of racing being rather stringent on the big time. Long ago the great racing writer O'Neil Sevier wrote of a New York race:

"The strangler aboard Rover Boy rode as if both he and his mount were owned by a bookmaking syndicate. Leaving the gate tardily, he was caught in three blind switches before the first turn was reached. After that he merely failed to improve his position. I strongly recommend he go back to walking hots, rather than riding coolers."

Such things don't happen often nowadays. More to the point of the present book, those things that *do* happen will not catch a good handicapper unaware frequently enough to necessitate red ink. The good handicapper knows his favorite racetrack like an owl knows his tree. He knows which stables are which and which jockeys are which. Above all, he knows which horses are which by studying the past-performance charts.

But how can he tell anything about a stable's present intentions or a jockey's attitude from the past performances? Read on and find out. Today's intentions flow directly from the horse's past history. The past-performance records and other published information tell a lot.

The casual racegoer attends the carousel only a few times a year. Can he hope to match wits with handicappers who are there every day? Yes he can. A good handicapper who is at the track every day will know more about individual horses, stables, and jockeys than someone who relies entirely on published statistics. But the occasional horseplayer can get by handsomely. This book tells how.

19

TWO / The Making of a Jockey—And What the Jockey Makes

TODAY'S ATHLETES ARE THE BEST IN THE HISTORY OF THE WORLD. High school children run and swim faster than Olympic champions used to. College baseball pitchers have better stuff than major leaguers used to. Professional golfers lose modern tournaments while hitting the ball farther and no less accurately than Open champions used to.

Not only are today's champions better than the champions of the past, but today's average player—of almost any game—is incomparably better than the average player of the past. Only two major exceptions come to mind. One is boxing, which has deteriorated because hardly anyone takes it up today. The other exception is Thoroughbred horse racing, because too many people go in for it now, and there are not enough good horses, good trainers, and good jockeys to go around.

In the era of the walrus mustache, ankle-length skirt, and parasol, Thoroughbred racing was the summer occupation of a curious coalition of socialites, lifelong horsemen, professional gamblers, and miscellaneous bums. They conducted their frequently felonious affairs without external supervision. A day's program consisted of six or seven races. The tempo was leisurely. Purses were small.

But the quality of the average horse was, by today's standards, extraordinarily high. The objective of every breeder was to produce animals capable of going the long distances that were and are the ultimate test of Thoroughbred class. To go such distances against worthy competition, a horse had to be physically sound. Foals and yearlings with conformations below standard were systematically weeded out. This was done because (a) such animals showed no promise of ever winning much at the track, and (b) there was no sense in allowing them to produce physically inferior foals of their own. The phrase "improvement of the breed" was honored on a wide scale. These high standards were unavoidable: the competition in big-time racing was keen, and there was no place in it for inferior stock.

Horses—even mediocre ones—rested during the winter, when the only races were in the minor leagues of Havana, Tijuana, and New Orleans. When northern racing resumed in the spring, the horses were fresh and fit. The record of the great Exterminator is a good case in point. The first race of his life did not occur until June of his two-year-old season (1917). He had three more by the end of July and then was rested. His next start came nine months later in the 1918 Kentucky Derby. He won. Nowadays a two-year-old as promising as Exterminator was *may* be coddled and withheld from competition until June of his first racing year, but it is not likely. Moreover, he probably will compete for hundreds of thousands of dollars in purse money during the rest of that year. Then he probably will run his heart out in the big-money winter races at Florida or California tracks and break down forever before he gets to the Derby. It happens every year.

With racing a twelve-month sport, the mutuel machines gobbling up billions of dollars in bets, and purses larger than anyone except a lunatic would have predicted twenty years ago, the prevailing emphasis is on quantity, not quality. If you can stand some statistics, the following table will give you an idea what has happened.

These figures show the growth of Thoroughbred racing from a colorful, slightly raffish sport into a major industry. The professional gamblers are still around, but there are fewer of them, and their influence has been reduced to the vanishing point, partly by the cops and partly by the substitution of pari-mutuels for the larcenous man-to-man handbook type of betting. The coalition of socialites and lifelong horsemen persists and has been fortified to some extent by an influx of newly rich businessmen and other doers with a yen for the glamor of the turf. Neither the riches of these folk nor the know-how of their high-priced employees is sufficient to produce enough sound animals to fill the thousands of races that take place every year.

YEAR	RACING DAYS	TOTAL RACES	TOTAL PURSES	NEW FOALS
1915	839	5,454	$2,853,037	2,120
1946	3,020	23,940	$49,291,024	6,579
1965	5,283	47,335	$126,463,984	18,420
1973	6,906	62,270	$233,921,194	26,014

The demand for low-grade horseflesh with which to keep the mutuel windows busy is being met by industrialized breeding farms. Their principal merchandise is woefully polluted stock, capable of brief speed but seldom able to run farther than three-quarters of a mile. Under the stress of racing on modern, speeded-up tracks these crooked-legged creatures tend to break down rapidly. The tendency is accelerated by the mercilessly unsporting attitudes and wretchedly unskillful methods of many trainers and owners. Scores of incompetent trainers and bubble-headed owners have been attracted by the gold and glory available in this growing business. One rarely hears the expression "improvement of the breed" anymore, except in mockery.

But the crowds love it and the track proprietors love it and the politicians love it. In 1973 the states extracted $339 million in tax revenues from Thoroughbred racing, compared with $6 million in 1934. The trend toward more taxation seems irreversible. An accompanying, quite inevitable trend is toward more and more inducements to gamble or, as the boys say, more "betting opportunities." More "opportunities" means more betting, more revenue for the track, and more loot for the state treasury. So the six- or seven-race program has gone the way of the dodo. Programs now include nine or ten races, a daily double and perhaps a twin double, some exactas, quinellas, triple perfectas, and Lord knows what other invitations to waste money on slow horses.

New York's season opens in February and does not end until January, when it shuts down reluctantly, perhaps to cool off the seats. Charles Town, Lincoln Downs, and other hungry northern tracks seem to specialize in races run by cripples through snowstorms on frozen ground. The only major racing state with genuine restraint is, of all places, California, which limits Santa Anita and Hollywood Park to annual meetings of ninety-five and seventy-five days respectively. Either of those two plants would be a far more appropriate setting for winter racing than the wind tunnel at Aqueduct.

All right. Agreed. Racing has deteriorated and will undoubtedly get even worse before it gets better. Strangely enough, this is no serious obstacle to a good handicapper. In some instances it is an actual advantage.

For example, although modern racing ruins good horses before their time, it has not abolished good horses. At major tracks during the summer of the year, it is unusual if the smart handicapper does not discover swift, consistent, relatively pain-free horses in at least two races a day. The winning chances of such animals, when they are in shape, are often improved considerably by the lackluster quality and disheveled condition of the horses they run against. Time and time again, the good handicapper goes to the paddock with two horses in mind and discovers that he can eliminate one of them because it simply is in no condition to run its best race.

All this has a great deal to do with our subject—jockeys. The demand for more horses, even though breeders cannot possibly supply good ones in the desired profusion, has naturally brought with it a demand for more jockeys to ride all the extra stock at all the new tracks. Oddly, good jockeys have been at least as hard to find as good horses. The reasons are fascinating.

The American male is much taller and heavier than he used to be.

But jockeys must be small. So the pool of individuals physically qualified for the work is more shallow than ever. Moreover, the training given to fledgling riders is much like the training given to modern horses—superficial and hurried. To say that the average modern jockey is less than an expert horseman is to put the case mildly. The late Jules Wessler, a highly respected trainer and former jockey, once observed:

"Nowadays any undersized kid with an athletic build and competitive spirit has a fair chance of becoming a rider. With most races at six furlongs and with the emphasis on mass-production breeding for cheap speed, not much is asked of a kid beyond some ability to break a horse out of the gate, steer it and whip it. And, oh, do they whip!

"In the old days you couldn't afford to put a boy into a race until he was reasonably well schooled. The other jocks would have made mincemeat of him and your horse would have wound up hanging over the infield fence like a towel. A kid had to know horses before he was even allowed to sit on one, much less ride it in a race. He'd muck out stalls and carry water and walk hots and learn some respect for the individuality of horses. Maybe within a year you'd let him sit on one while it strolled under the shed or jogged around a walking ring. If the boy enjoyed his work and the horses took kindly to him, he'd finally get to gallop a few in the morning.

"By the time you let him ride a horse in a race he might have been around for two or three or four years. He'd have developed a notion of how to break from the gate, how to judge the pace of a race, how to take hold of a horse and rate it, how to move with the horse's own running rhythm so as to be an asset instead of a burden, how to use his hands on the horse's neck to push it ahead in a drive, how to use the whip without beating the animal to shreds. And *when* to use the whip, which was seldom, compared to the flogging they do today. And the kid would have learned how to handle the reins smoothly to get a rank or frightened or confused horse to change leads going around a turn, and how to handle a horse which tended to lug in or bear out. And he would have seen enough races and talked enough racing to have a fair idea how to keep his mount out of the switches, and how to protect himself against the rough riding that was standard practice."

A new jockey was never put on a potential winner. The old-time trainers used to ride him in fifty or sixty races before they let him break his maiden. But when he finally won, he was ready to win again and again, because he was well on his way to mastering his trade. A year or so after his first victory he would lose the weight allowance granted to apprentice riders. Then, as now, the trainers had to decide whether they wanted his services with the extra five pounds he now would be putting on their horses. In the present era, most young riders absolutely disappear from major tracks after losing the apprentice weight allowance and becoming journeymen.

"The weight allowance is the only reason trainers have for using most of those kids," said Wessler. "They lose the allowance and they get no more work. But when jockeys had to go through the tough schooling that made *jockeys* of them, the loss of the apprentice allowance was seldom the end of the line."

It should be emphasized that there is more to riding Thoroughbreds than the kind of instructions the beginner gets, or the kind of experience he accumulates in actual races. There is such a thing as riding talent. Horsemen become inarticulate when asked to define or describe this talent. Most of them say that it consists of "the ability to get more out of more horses than other riders can." But how? Why?

Horsemen also speak admiringly of "strong" riders. This refers not to the jock's musculature but to his ability to hold horses together in the homestretch and run strong finishes with them. Again how? Why?

Ted Atkinson, known as "The Slasher" because his whip was rarely at rest, was the country's leading rider in 1944 and 1946. He always seemed to me to be a strong, talented rider, but surprisingly few horsemen agree.

"There's a lot of politics in big-time racing," an expert explains. "Atkinson was a good rider but no better than dozens of others who rode against him. What he was great at was talking. He was an indefatigable promoter. He always had a good agent, like Goldie Mitchell or the late Nick Huff, and he also hustled mounts for himself. The guy who gets the most good mounts wins the most races, and that helps him get more good mounts. Plenty of boys better than Atkinson didn't get the mounts and didn't get the breaks that bring more mounts."

Nick Wall, another former national riding champion and a topnotch jockey for years, remembers his old rival Atkinson as superbly talented. "Ted did a lot of unorthodox and apparently incorrect things on a horse," says Wall, "but he had a great gift for winning races. He'd ride with a slack hold—the reins so loose you'd expect that the horse's head would drop and that it would begin to flounder any second. But the horses ran for him and nobody knew why. He'd hook you at the eighth pole and beat you, and the next day he'd do it again, three or four times. And he'd do it when you thought you had the better horse. And when you thought the race was won for you. They called him 'The Slasher' and a lot of the old-timers criticized the frequency with which he used the whip. But a funny thing about it: I never knew him to leave a mark on a horse."

So Atkinson got more than the expected from his mounts. This means he was a good, "strong" rider. Was this talent related to his notably high intelligence? Possibly, in the sense that he was smart enough to study the game. But some of the greatest riders have been impossible dumbbells when walking around on their own feet in the world at large. Some have been actual morons, impervious to much knowledge beyond what they had learned about riding races.

Let us then forget intellect. Good riders don't need any. As nearly as I can make out after innumerable conversations at the track, a jockey's talent is compounded of courage, extreme alertness, fast reflexes, stubbornly competitive spirit, physical condition as good as that of professional athletes in any other sport, and, above all, a sensitivity to the varying needs and capacities of horses. Having obtained adequate instruction and experience, such a jockey develops powers of anticipation that enable him to exploit running opportunities at the very instant they arise during a race. The same powers help him to avoid trouble by running away from it, pulling outside it, or backing off even before it occurs. This kind of judgment becomes most valuable in the big stakes races run at longer distances. The top-notch jockey's feeling for his horse, for the pace of the race, and for the state of the competition tells him the exact time to make the moves that win the big ones.

Of the almost 2,500 jockeys who rode in this country during 1974, not more than twenty qualify as first-rate. This is to say that not more than twenty are both *sufficiently* and *consistently* alert, courageous, quick, stubbornly competitive, and in prime physical shape. These twenty or fewer riders can be counted on to get the best from almost every horse they ride. Day in and day out, they can be relied on to exercise the superior judgment that wins races. Day in and day out, furthermore, they can be relied on to get the choicest mounts.

It now sounds simple, but it is not. In Chapter One I pointed out that anyone who bets on jockeys will lose money. There have been entire months, and perhaps entire seasons, when a bet on every one of Laffit Pincay's mounts would have shown a tiny profit for a huge investment. Other jockeys frequently reward system players with a profit over the course of a week or two. But in the long haul, disaster awaits such a bettor. Let me now give more reasons for this than I offered earlier. One is that some of the top twenty riders compete against each other in the same races, and there can be no more than one winner per race. A more fundamental reason is that, at any given time, *any of perhaps a hundred other riders may be riding like champions.* The good form may persist for weeks and months. Riders of this kind also get hot mounts. In many races they get better mounts than Pincay, Shoemaker, or Angel Cordero do.

To explain the phenomenon of the temporarily hot apprentice or temporarily hot journeyman who, mounted on live horses, beats the best jockeys in the land over and over again before lapsing into mediocrity or worse, it is necessary to analyze some of the pressures to which jockeys are subjected. Only the greatest—and the luckiest —can withstand these pressures well enough to reach the top and remain there for years, getting their share of good mounts and deserving to get them. Other riders, like the hundred or so mentioned above, enjoy briefer periods when everything goes well, they win races, and are in demand.

What, then, prevents them from maintaining this high standard over longer periods of time? What accounts for the slumps from which some of them never recover?

"You've got to have your mind on your work," says a top-notch jockey who prefers not to be named. "You've got to be free in your mind so that you can concentrate on what you're doing. It's like shooting pool or playing poker. If you get overconfident or if something is bothering you, it's going to hurt your game. In big-time racing, if this happens and you begin to lose races you should have won, you're in big trouble. Nobody wants to use you anymore."

The things that prevent jockeys from getting their work done properly will sound familiar to men in other fields. One of the principal difficulties is immaturity. An adolescent who makes $50,000 in a year may decide that he is king of the world. By the time the resultant sloppiness has ruined his reputation as a rider, it is too late. Another difficulty is fear. After a serious spill or two, only a remarkably brave man will return to the races with the daring that he had before his hospitalization. But daring is essential in big-time racing, and boys who lack it get no work.

Another rather widespread problem in the trade is unhappy marriage. I do not know whether mismating is more frequent among jockeys than among ribbon clerks, but I am sure that the reasons for the mismating are not the same in the two crafts. A successful young jockey makes a lot more money than a ribbon clerk. He has access to young ladies who combine extreme physical beauty with a taste for the high life and a yen to spend dough as fast as a man can earn it. Let the jockey hit the almost inevitable slump and he may find (as hundreds have found) that Darling's ardor has begun to cool, although she is more than willing to let him go into hock with gamblers and loan sharks to raise mink money for her. The domestic dissension and financial difficulties involved in this sort of thing show themselves in the rider's work. His slump intensifies because he is below par. The word gets around the track, and the trainers treat him like a smallpox case.

Several seasons ago I asked one of the smartest trainers in the business why he and others never used a certain rider who had once been among the national leaders. The jockey was still young but was getting only infrequent assignments and rarely rode a live horse. "The boy is as good as he ever was," said the trainer. "Maybe better. But he got into a slump over that broad. Then he began betting on horses. So now he's in debt to too many people. If I put him on a horse that has a chance to win, he'll be on the telephone right away, tipping off his creditors, and they'll bet enough to drive the odds down. Who needs it?"

Not many jockeys get such reputations as gamblers. Those who do find themselves, of course, in permanent trouble at the major tracks. Other kinds of difficulties are much more often the reasons for a jockey's loss of favor among trainers.

"Look," says a jockey. "You get going good and you buy an expensive house and a couple of expensive cars and then you run into bad luck for a while and you don't have a dime, but the mortgage is still there, and the wife and kids are still there, and the anxiety has you by the throat but good. So a trainer decides to take a chance on you because of what you've done for him in the past. Maybe the opportunity is just what you need to get started again as a winner. But just as likely it's not. There's such a thing as trying too hard, you know. If the race is not just a *race* but a matter of life and death, you may blow it. You may be overanxious. In a *race*, you have to be as cool as possible, as opportunistic as possible. But if your whole damned career—your whole life—seems to be riding with you, you may make the one or two riding mistakes that louse you up. The trainer won't hire you again."

And then there is drink. A few of America's better riders have suffered that problem and have licked it. Most who have had the problem have not licked it. The great Buddy Ensor died a panhandling wino, his face covered with running sores. Carrol Shilling, probably one of the greatest of all time, perished of malnutrition and exposure under a horse van across the street from Belmont Park's main entrance. One of the best of present-day riders fought a heroic battle against alcohol after almost permitting it to ruin his career. He is now getting mounts every day and riding in good form. His achievement is exceedingly rare. Other fine jockeys who should be winning big purses this year, because they are still young and won such purses in recent years, are scarcely heard from anymore. Booze.

The reason most frequently cited for a rider's tumble from the top ranks is the difficulty hundreds of them have in keeping their weight down. Many jockeys have to torture themselves in sweatboxes, eating only one small meal a day and deliberately heaving any other food they swallow. They risk trainers' displeasure if they come in a pound or two overweight. It takes stern ambition for a young man to subject himself to rigors of that sort year after year. It also can wreck his health. Naturally, this diminishes his efficiency aboard a horse. A man whose head is spinning with the dizziness of hunger and dehydration is simply not able to ride properly.

Jockeys, like other denizens of the track, are chasers after jackpots. They all start out thinking that they can make a couple of hundred thousand dollars a year like those in the top ranks. During the glamorous victorious year or so of apprenticeship which some of them experience, the dough is bigger than they've ever seen before. Then comes the end of the apprentice weight allowance, and the bottom drops out. Or the bottom drops out later, for one or another of the reasons we have mentioned. And where does this leave the jockey? In bad shape.

The Jockeys' Guild, which has been trying, without sensational success, to negotiate a measure of financial security for riders, reports that half of all jockeys earn $5,000 a year or less. A good, hustling exercise boy can make twice as much in the mornings, without risking his neck in competition. At big-time tracks, the rider of a winning horse is paid $50. He gets $40 for coming in second, $30 for third, and $25 for a losing ride. It also is customary, and therefore taken for granted, that the rider of the winning horse gets 10 percent of the purse.

That, of course, is where the big money comes in. When Ron Turcotte won the 1973 Kentucky Derby on Secretariat, the winning share of the purse was $155,050, of which the rider got $15,505. Two weeks later, the same horse won $129,900 in the Preakness—$12,990 more in Ron's pocket. And when Secretariat completed his triple crown by running off with the Belmont Stakes and $90,120, Turcotte drew down $9,012. In those three races, the Canadian rider made $37,507—considerably more than many other journeyman jockeys get in an entire year.

During 1973, Turcotte and the 29 other leading money riders in North America brought their employers more than $56 million in purses. That is, about 1 percent of all riders won 24 percent of all purses. Of the $178 million in purse money available to the 2,500 other jockeys, about $106 million represented the winning ends of purses from which riders draw the coveted 10 percent. This meant that $10.6 million in bonuses was distributed among 2,500 riders—an average of around $4,000 each. Averages are deceptive. More than half of those 2,500 riders did not make even that much in competition.

Take Pete Anderson, one of the best in the world. In 1972 he won only six races, grossing $40,008 in purse money. He was forty-one at the time but still a powerful factor on a two-year-old or on grass or on any horse trying to navigate around two turns. His main handicaps were chronic weight problems, a penchant for abrading the sensitive egos of owners and trainers, and, not least, a reputation for rough riding. In short, he could win no popularity contests. So Pete got only 52 rides during 1972 and was lucky if he earned $5,000 that way.

Terry Bove, only thirty-one, had once been the leading apprentice rider in New York, but in 1972 he rode only 27 winners in 302 attempts for total purses of $105,804 and less take-home pay than a fry cook's. Another former apprentice star was Ernie Cardone. In 1966, when the first edition of this book was written, the New York youngster was the hottest new rider in the country. Trainers elbowed each other for the privilege of boosting him onto live mounts. He rode 1,297 times, winning 240 for an elegant average of .185 and purses of $1,275,111. But it all slowed down after Ernie lost the "bug"—the asterisk which appears next to the apprentice rider's name, signifying that the stable gets weight off its horse for using the services of a green kid. Where once Ernie had been credited with the well-rounded talents required for a long and successful career in competition, he now became an object of doubt. He became unfashionable. The owner was no longer thrilled by the notion of having Cardone aboard. Horsemen complained that he was a slow learner, or not quite strong enough. No longer helped by the apprentice's weight allowance, Ernie got fewer live mounts. And in time he got scarcely any mounts at all.

In 1972, although he was no less expert and no less resolute than during his glory years, Ernie Cardone rode only 10 winners, bringing his employers $78,332 in purse money and probably making less than $10,000 in the process. And Willie Lester was in even worse straits. Aged forty and as quick out of the gate, as wily in traffic, and as strong in the stretch as any rider in the land, Lester had just about abandoned hope of recovering his place at the top of the profession. It had been years since Lester's heyday, but everyone in the business knew that no better rider existed, once allowances were made for the rustiness that comes from lack of competitive activity.

Preparing this book back in 1966, I wrote that Willie had won three of his most recent seven starts and had been out of the money only twice. The figures were impressive, but they did not help. Willie was out of style. By 1972, as I was saying, he had just about given it up. He went to the post 56 times and won once.

For the horseplayer, the point of all this is that a jockey cannot win races unless he gets winning horses to ride. That Ernie Cardone and Pete Anderson won only a handful of races during 1972 does not mean that they were detrimental to their losing mounts. Indeed, Pete did a little better in 1973, winning 17 times and bringing $311,586 to the owners. And in 1974 he won stakes races on Cannonade, helping establish the animal as a leading contender in that year's Kentucky Derby. But the stable shelved the veteran before Derby Day, reasoning with considerable logic that Angel Cordero would be a better risk, having been much more active. As history shows, Cordero and Cannonade won the roses and Pete Anderson burned more bridges by unloading sardonic comment about Cannonade's managers.

As this book proceeds, the reader will see that the choice of rider often tells as much about the chances of the horses as does anything else in the animal's record. The trainer with a live horse tends, quite understandably, to go to the rider who (a) has been winning recently and often and (b) will please the owner. More on this in due course.

THREE / The Jockey and the Trainer and the Race

IN 1972 AND 1973, BOBBY FRANKEL SADDLED 954 HORSES, OF WHICH 255 won. His winning average of 26.7 percent was unapproached by any other major-league trainer who started as many horses during those two years. Indeed, the only horseman who surpassed that average in the big time was the peerless Frank Y. Whiteley, Jr., who specializes in quality not quantity. Whiteley sent only 223 horses to the post during 1972 and 1973, winning 61 times for an average of 27.4 percent.

What comes to mind when somebody says "trainer"? For most of us the word conjures up the image of a leathery-faced yokel, a Walter Brennan type with manure on his shoes, a kindly old gaffer who is always muttering, "Whoa, girl, steady there." Some good trainers fit this description. Bobby Frankel does not. He is strictly urban. He seems vaguely displaced when you find him outdoors. Yet the open air is his element. That's where his horses win all those races.

The Brooklynite started as a lowly stable hand, employed by stalwarts such as Buddy Jacobson and Bill Corbellini. When he set forth on his own, it took him a while to roll. In 1966 he had only 21 starters. Five of them won—an elegant percentage. In 1967 he won 9, and in 1968 he really began to cook, winning 36 of 165 starts. That was the year in which he claimed Baitman for a trifling

$15,000. The gallant gray went on to win more than ten times the purchase price. Another Frankel claim, Barometer (also for $15,000), proceeded to take the Suburban Handicap and about $112,000 in purses.

When New York racing bogged down in labor disputes, Frankel and his cavalry decamped to Southern California, where he promptly broke all records for consistent victory. In his first fling at Hollywood Park, he started 180 times and won a phenomenal 60. He became a fixture in the West, characteristically leading every meeting and returning to New York only for brief visits. If the American horseplayer has a best friend, it may be Frankel.

The aspiring handicapper cannot really understand the role of the rider without peering behind the scenes at the trainer. How does one account for the prolonged and conspicuous success of a Bobby Frankel? Or a Frank Whiteley? Or an H. Allen Jerkens? Or a Charlie Whittingham? Do they know some secrets? Do horses talk to them?

The job of a trainer is to enter ready runners in suitable races. If he does only that, he cannot fail to win a substantial percentage of his starts. Hundreds and hundreds of horsemen *know* enough about their trade to get a horse ready and find a suitable race, but only a few *do* these two things consistently enough to achieve the good winning percentage.

There is a secret, all right. And it has more to do with human beings than with horses. Real horsemanship demands patience. But patience costs money. Patience means waiting for the minor injury to heal, or for the bad habit to give way to the good. Patience means waiting for the right spot on the right kind of racing strip. So patience creates difficulties in an environment where almost everyone is obsessed with short-range results.

The typical track management is impatient. It would rather not assign stall space to horses being rested by patient trainers. Management wants those horses to be racing, ready or not, in races that may not be suitable. If the horse is idle, nobody can bet on it, and bets are what enlarge the pari-mutuel handle. Marginal trainers whose horses are owned by persons without great influence are told in no uncertain terms to race those horses or ship out.

Unless a horse is a champion, he is sooner or later treated as an expendable item. His long-term well-being runs second to the immediate appetites of men. Indeed, recent racing history names some actual champions who have been ruined by being sent after the extra dollar when not in top condition. When something like that happens, the owner and his unhappy trainer are usually lauded as great sportsmen willing to take a chance with a horse rather than disappoint the public. Hooey. No great sportsman would risk harming a horse. And sportsmanship is questionable when it involves seducing the public into betting on a horse whose condition is below par.

Naturally, the owners of racehorses do not want to ruin their own animals and diminish the value of their investments. But life is complicated. In their own way, owners are subject to pressures as severe as those they impose on the trainers.

If the owner is new to the game (as many are in a field notorious for quick turnover), he usually craves quick action for his buck. When he brings friends, family, and customers to his tax-deductible clubhouse box, he wants them to see his racing colors in action. And he wants to be photographed in the winner's circle. If Trainer A can't keep that promise in a hurry, Trainer B is ready with brighter promises. The competition is fierce. And Trainers A, B, and Z have little choice but to gamble on the outcome. You can't win races and please owners with inactive horses. So you send unready ones and pray.

Owners more experienced in the sport—including some whose great-grandparents and all intervening forebears also were in racing —are not always easier to get along with. Some tend to be opinionated. The trainer who survives in their employ is as likely to be a top-notch diplomat as a top-notch horseman.

Call Bobby Frankel, Frank Whiteley, Allen Jerkens, and Charlie Whittingham lucky. They are not burdened with such problems. They handle horses in the best ways they know how, and they win decent percentages of their starts every year. Their owners respect them and leave them alone. Whittingham, in particular, has dealt successfully with some of the most demanding (to put it mildly) horse owners without yielding an inch—and has made them like it. So a consistently successful trainer is not just lucky. He has character.

The owner of Cougar II was quoted in *Sports Illustrated* as wishing Charlie took her advice more often. She said that she would happily give the animal to another trainer if she could find a better one. But she could find none better.

"I've been around them all from coast to coast," said Bill Shoemaker to *Sports Illustrated*'s Whitney Tower, "and there's not a finer horseman in the U.S. He understands his horses and treats them like athletes."

He understands the need for patience, and no power on earth can pressure him into moving prematurely with a horse. The same may be said of his eastern peers, Whiteley and Jerkens, and that genius of the assembly line, Bobby Frankel.

Frankel's operation is different from the others, since he starts so very many animals. To maintain a high winning average, it is necessary for him to (a) claim relatively sound horses when they are just about ready to win and (b) spot them where they can get the job done. He sometimes does this by dropping them in class. Just as often, he moves them up in class, having found the hole card—the matter of shoeing or diet or training exercise needed to transform a mediocre claimer into a big winner.

In one sense Frankel may be said to specialize in taking other people's well-conditioned horses away from them. There is nothing unethical about it. Claiming races are the game's bread and butter. Any horse entered in such a race may be claimed (bought at a predetermined and publicly posted price) by any bona fide horseman. If such contests were not prevalent, sub-par animals would be unable to win occasional races and earn their keep—and racing would be unable to present all the programs it does.

Because any horse entered in a claiming race can be taken from its owner, the barns are careful not to put $10,000 stock into races programmed for $5,000 stock. The $10,000 horse would win, but the victory would be hollow, because someone surely would grab the bargain for $5,000. This natural reluctance to give something for nothing explains why claiming races almost always present quite evenly matched horses—horses of approximately equal quality.

So there is nothing wrong when Bobby Frankel or Dave Vance or José Martin or other haltermen reach in and claim other people's property. The best of them make brilliant choices. A horse will run eighth, sixth, fifth, and fourth in its most recent starts and today runs out of the money again, yet—lo and behold—a Frankel or Martin or Vance claims it for $10,000 and wins with it next time out.

"He runs them off other people's training," goes the customary backstretch criticism of a successful claiming horseman. "He watches everything like a hawk. He knows when a horse is finally rounding into shape. And then he lowers the boom and gets two, three, five, eight decent races out of the hide."

And he knows whom to boost into the irons when the horse is ready to win. As a rule the most successful trainers and riders find security in each other. Bobby Frankel prefers Laffit Pincay, leading money-winning jockey of the time and one of the best of any time. Charlie Whittingham has first call on another immortal, Bill Shoemaker. At this writing, Frank Whiteley inclines toward the clever Jacinto Vasquez. In all three cases the feeling is mutual. What rider in his right mind would not choose to accept mounts from these barns?

But there is more to it than that. Allen Jerkens is fond of observing, "If I send out fit horses, it makes little difference who steers them. If they aren't ready, no jockey can make them win."

When the stick-in-the-muds of the backstretch were treating women jockeys like typhoid carriers, Jerkens employed the talented Robyn C. Smith on winner after winner. When John Ruane fell into general disfavor as one reputed to be quick out of the gate but weak in the homestretch, Jerkens continued to use him and got many a fine stretch drive from him. During 1974, Jerkens' first forty winners at Aqueduct and Belmont Park were piloted by eleven different jockeys—an astounding number of switches for a first-rate stable. The riders included not only Robyn Smith, Ruane, Jorge Velasquez, Mike Hole, Eddie Maple, Angel Cordero, and Daryl Montoya, some of them national leaders and the others obviously in fine form at the time. But Jerkens also assigned winners to struggling riders. Bill Mayorga had been on New England's leaky-roof circuit for years after failing to set New York afire as a youth. Jaime Arellano had displayed promise but was not yet accepted as a top-notcher. James Long was a new apprentice. And John Czarnecki was the newest of all—and Jerkens boosted him onto a winner the very first time the youngster rode in a real race.

Some like to argue that Jerkens' approach demonstrates the unimportance of the rider. I prefer to see it as evidence that (a) New York is cluttered with highly competent riders and (b) Jerkens knows which of the local jocks is suitable for his horse. No doubt Cordero would have won with the animal driven by Czarnecki. It simply ran away from the rest of the field. I am positive that Jerkens would not have been so ready to use Czarnecki on some of the horses that won tough races for Cordero, Velasquez, Smith, Ruane, or Hole.

It is worth bearing in mind that the best horse in the race benefits from the attentions of a competent rider. The right rider is insurance. When a handicapper discovers that two animals in a race seem to stand out from the rest of the field, his final decision may well be affected by the knowledge that one of these contenders is trained by a Dave Vance and ridden by a Darrell McHargue, whereas the other not only is being piloted by an apprentice who has never managed to bring it home in front but is trained by a gent with a frighteningly low percentage of winners.

This is not, by the way, a suggestion that the reader bet on trainers instead of on horses, the way other suckers bet on jockeys. In good handicapping, the horse's record is the chief factor. All else is merely supplementary data. But data of that kind help make the difference between sound handicapping and indifferent handicapping.

The reader now asks how in the world he is to know who the smart trainers are if he doesn't go to the track every day and become part of its social structure. The answer is that all the material he really needs is available in print. The most important is found in *The American Racing Manual,* published annually by the *Daily Racing Form,* 731 Plymouth Court, Chicago, Ill. 60605. The *Form* and the track's daily programs publish other useful information on the subject. In the *Manual,* one sees how the trainers did last year. In the daily publications, one discovers how they are doing this season.

The good handicapper is keenly interested in the consistency with which a trainer saddles winners. As most readers probably know, but as I had better digress to point out, the customary definition of consistency in a *horse* is its ability to win about one of every five races in which it is entered. Many of the best bets you will ever make will be on horses which qualify as consistent but which are overlooked by the crowd because of supposedly poor current form. On the other hand, lucrative bets also are made on inconsistent horses that happen to have an edge in basic class or current form or sheer speed. So consistency is merely *one* of the numerous interrelated factors that the smart player weighs in evaluating a horse's chances. The subject will be surveyed in depth later on. But when we consider the *trainer,* consistency becomes a paramount factor.

As far as I am concerned, a trainer unable to get into the winner's circle about once in every five attempts is too inconsistent to command utmost confidence. The question arises with particular meaning when his horse faces stern opposition from one trained by a truly consistent trainer.

What makes one trainer consistent and another not? The difference may not always be attributable to real differences in ability. A trainer can't win unless he has winning horses to train, just as a jockey can't win unless he has winning horses to ride. Regardless of the sympathy we may feel for victims of life's injustice, we are

40

careful about betting money on them. In short, a trainer's consistency record, past and present, tells us something we need to know about his chances in today's race.

Here are the trainers who qualified as outstandingly consistent in big-time racing during 1973:

	TOTAL STARTS	WINS	WINNING PERCENTAGE
J. Bowes Bond	268	56	20.8
Sunshine Calvert	92	21	22.8
Lou Cavalaris, Jr.	362	80	22
Dick Dutrow	783	195	24.9
Bobby Frankel	505	143	28
Tom Harraway	67	15	22.4
Dick Hazelton	816	199	24
Bob Hilton	456	100	21.9
Dom Imprescia	193	39	20.2
H. Allen Jerkens	405	83	20
King T. Leatherbury	801	176	22
Frank J. McManus	146	30	20.5
Jim Morgan	399	106	26.6
Eddie Navarro	101	22	21.8
Jim O'Bryant	152	40	26.3
John W. Russell	223	50	22.4
Joe Trovato	398	84	21.1
Dave Vance	791	183	23.1
Katherine Voss	141	28	20
Art Warner	239	48	20
Charlie Whittingham	423	85	20

A list like that requires a certain amount of hair-splitting. Among the authentically dependable trainers who missed it by a percentage point or two were Tony Basile, Junie Bresnahan, Elliott Burch, Henry Clark, Reggie Cornell, Frank Gomez, Karl Grusmark, Steve Ippolito, Jim Maloney José Martin, John Nerud, Lefty Nickerson, John Parisella, Lou Rondinello, Larry Rose, John Tammaro, Noble Threewitt, and Arnold Winick. But the point is made: Of the more than 7,500 individuals licensed to train Thoroughbreds in the United States, only 20 managed to win 20 percent or more of their starts while engaged principally in racing on major circuits. Another 30 or so managed to accomplish the good percentage on minor tracks.

The studious horseplayer who puts his *American Racing Manual* and *Daily Racing Form* to work will find that the list of truly consistent trainers changes only slightly from year to year. When used in combination with the "Leading Trainers" tabulation published daily in racing papers and track programs, the annual percentages help the player to know who's who and, to some extent, what's what. These, after all, are the trainers with the reliable horses. These are the trainers to whom the successful riders gravitate, wanting to ride more winners. These are the trainers who not only are *trying* to win at every possible opportunity but are good enough to get far better than average results.

A trainer on the 20 percent list whose percentages become somewhat less impressive in the next year's edition of *The American Racing Manual* may nevertheless appear in the daily tabulation as one of the leading figures at the current meeting. In that case, you know he's pretty much his old self. If he disappears from the daily tabulation and his *Manual* statistics also fall markedly below the cherished 20 percent, it will pay to find out whether he has changed his place of employment. He may now be serving owners who race substandard horses. We shall return to this question when we review the Plus Factors in handicapping, at which point I shall show how to put the information to work.

A similar body of information which the player will find highly useful is much harder to come by. It concerns the trainers' percentages of winning favorites and is most revealing of their talents and temperaments. As the reader knows, favorites in the betting win almost exactly one-third of all races. The statistics stand up year in and year out. It may vary up or down in rather wide swings when measured over short periods of time. But at the end of a representative period, like a year, it will settle at just about exactly one winner for every three betting favorites. It seems to me that any trainer who saddles a large number of favorites and fails to win at least one time out of three is doing something wrong. Over the long season, there is no good reason why his favorites should not perform in a manner close to average. Indeed, if he is a truly reliable trainer, there is no reason why his favorites should not surpass the average and win at least 40 percent of the time.

The same consistent ability which enables the genuinely reliable trainer to win one in five starts accounts for his superior performances with favorites. Whether the horses trained by these men go to the post as favorites or not, they are usually in good running condition, are well placed as to distance, class, and weight, and are ridden by suitable jockeys. As favorites, therefore, they are less likely to be false choices and more likely to give the chalk players an authentic run for the money.

Every year the New York State Racing Commission files an annual report which shows, among numerous other things, how the trainers made out with those of their horses that ran as betting favorites at New York and Saratoga. Anybody who lives in New York and is interested in Thoroughbred racing should be sure to obtain a copy of this public document every year. It's worth the trouble. Players who live elsewhere should ask their own state racing authority whether it issues similar reports.

According to the New York Commission, the following trainers saddled at least fifteen betting favorites at Aqueduct, Belmont and Saratoga during 1973 and achieved a winning percentage higher than the usual average of 33:

	FAVORITES	WINS	PERCENTAGE
Laz Barrera	61	25	41
Elliott Burch	51	22	43
John Campo	99	35	35
Reggie Cornell	19	10	53
Steve DiMauro	33	12	36
Bobby Dotter	16	7	44
Mike Freeman	23	11	48
Tom Gullo	41	14	34
Lenny Imperio	27	11	41
Allen Jerkens	99	43	43
Phil Johnson	44	16	36

Tommy Kelly	28	10	36
Lucien Laurin	39	18	46
Roger Laurin	32	12	38
Jim Maloney	15	9	60
Frank Martin	152	54	36
Mack Miller	29	10	34
John Nerud	40	16	40
Lefty Nickerson	59	23	39
John Parisella	83	29	35
Bill Resseguet	18	7	39
Woody Stephens	40	14	35
Howard Tesher	17	7	41
Jim Toner	18	8	44
Joe Trovato	60	27	45
Sid Watters	18	7	39

Needless to say, the horseplayer who likes the favorite in a race and finds that it is trained by one of the gents on this list can be somewhat easier in his mind about the wager.

Anyone who thinks that I have departed too far from our discussion of the relationship of jockeys to the winning and losing of horse races is urged to reconsider. The jockey can win the race only if the horse is capable of it. And to be capable of it, the horse must be expertly trained and entered against the kind of animals it can beat. Which brings us now to a most important aspect of handicapping. The trainer calls it "finding a spot" for his horse. The good horseplayer calls it "finding a playable race"—finding a spot for a bet, finding a race in which the abilities of the contestants are sufficiently evident to permit an informed guess as to a likely winner.

The trainer is at the track every day. He knows something about almost every animal in the place. If he is a good trainer, he knows more about his own horses than anyone else does. When he reads the condition book, looking for spots in which his horses will have good chances of catching purses, he does a kind of inside handicapping. He knows exactly what kinds of horses are going to be entered in each race. He can name the horses and the stables. He can make a tentative decision as to whether the race is, from his viewpoint, "playable."

The horseplayer is even better off. He does not have to decide days ahead of time whether to play a race or not. He can wait until the *Daily Racing Form* publishes the past-performance record of each entered animal.

Let us assume that the player's desire is to make as much money as possible. If this is *really* his wish, it is not diluted by a craving for gambling "action" or a yen to goof off for an afternoon at the track, betting indiscriminately. The player therefore will not go to the track (or will not bet any serious cash there) unless the weather is warm and the horses have been running there, or elsewhere on the regional circuit, for at least three weeks.

When I designed the conservative, high-percentage handicapping procedure contained in this book it was expressly for the purpose of overthrowing tradition and proving that the game could be beaten by anyone mentally and temperamentally capable of working at it. For years my mail has suggested that I achieved that objective. But it is quite clear that relatively few horseplayers are so obsessed with maximum winnings that they are willing to abide by some of the Spartan self-disciplines demanded in these pages.

For a good example, now that northern racing is available on a year-round basis, it is unrealistic to prescribe (as the first edition of this book did) that we go to the track only in nice weather. Let us now say that relatively dependable horses are being raced even in cold weather (the game having changed in adaptation to the extended seasons). And that a good handicapper can do nicely any time of year. And that only a fanatic (such as I used to be) would confine his action to the prime period between May and October.

Let me add, moreover, that this book's 1965 warnings against wet tracks also need no longer apply, provided that the handicapper makes sensible adjustments for the wetness. We'll get to that.

Regardless of individual attitudes toward beating the game, times of year, wetness of tracks, and the like, the first step in any proper handicapping method is to read the conditions of the race.

Some races are limited to the kinds of horses on which only madmen bet their money. Slow horses. Non-winners entered to be claimed. Untrustworthy horses. Nobody can hope to pick the least slow horse from a troop of slow ones often enough to make money at it. The reason they are slow is that something is wrong with them. Something is awry with the muscle or bone or the lungs or the heart or the temperament. And what has been wrong in the past can get worse today.

So the intelligent player looks for races with at least one horse with a respectable record, or at least a promising record.

Here are the main categories of races, and some observations about which of them are likely to be playable.

RACES FOR TWO-YEAR-OLDS

The best two-year-olds begin their careers in sprints of five, five-and-a-half, or six furlongs. In the East these races are called "Maiden Special Weights," and in California they are "Maiden"— differentiating them from the Maiden Claiming races programmed for cheaper juveniles. Attracting the best-bred youngsters from the best barns, the races are often difficult to handicap because they usually include several animals that have never run in public before. On rare occasions, however, one finds a field in which everything has been to the post in the past. Although none has won (which is what "maiden" means), one of them may have run the distance in better time than any of the others. Such a horse is usually a sound bet, even though the odds will be miserly.

On other infrequent occasions the field contains animals that not only have lost in their earlier efforts but have run the distance in poor time. (For a definition of "poor time" you have to familiarize yourself with the time figures at your own track.) But also entered will be a first-time starter that has been working out in spectacularly rapid style. If it's from a good barn and is to be ridden by a leading jockey, the first-timer is often a sound speculation, its competitors never having shown much.

Two-year-olds of less promise compete in maiden claiming sprints.

Their owners are ready to sell them, having written off their chances of winning big purses. These are the slowest horses and among the poorest investments at the track. The only time to hazard a bet is when one of the entrants is stepping down from the maiden-special-weights competition, in which its time figures were no worse than those of anything it will be running against today. The drop in class usually benefits a horse of this kind.

The foregoing references to time figures should not be taken as an indication that I think all horse races can be handicapped with a stopwatch. But two-year-old sprints can be. The horse that has run today's distance faster than all the others is the horse with the best chance today.

This notion is borne out most satisfactorily in allowance races for two-year-olds. Having won a maiden special weights, the horse no longer is eligible for such contests. His next rung on the competitive scale is an allowance affair against other previous winners. Sometimes a maiden is found in these events, and sometimes a first-time starter or two. Almost always, the ultimate winner is the animal that has run the distance most swiftly in previous efforts.

From the allowance race the next step upward for the good two-year-old is the stakes race. So long as these are at distances of five-and-a-half furlongs or less, the speed records suffice for handicapping. At longer distances it is best to pay attention to matters like pace (of which more later).

Before ending this discussion of two-year-olds, I should emphasize that good ones are just about the most reliable horses to be found anywhere. They are full of enthusiasm for their work. And since they run full tilt over the sprint distances at which most of them do most of their running, many of the subtleties of handicapping can be shelved. If the horse won his allowance race at five furlongs in faster time than his competitors ran theirs, he is highly likely to repeat the achievement today.

As to three-, four-, and four-and-a-half-furlong dashes which some tracks program for two-year-olds, once again the clock is the thing.

RACES FOR OLDER HORSES

Maiden Special Weights

A racehorse is supposed to win horse races once in a while. If it reaches the age of four without having demonstrated some ability, it is not worth betting on in competition at a major track. Certain socialite owners become attached to creatures of this kind and insist on entering them against superior competition, refusing to put them in claiming races. Forget 'em. The best prospect in races of this kind is a *three-year-old* that has not run more than three or four times, has been working out frequently, is from a good barn, and is being ridden by a jockey who wins races. The horse may not have run at all when it was two, or it may have run only once or twice. Perhaps it fell ill or was injured. If it has run a race or two in the last couple of weeks and has performed well, it could be a bet today.

Maiden Claimers

As observed earlier, it is foolhardy to try to find the least slow of a collection of slow horses. Three- and four-year-old non-winners entered to be claimed for less than $10,000 in this era of inflated prices are as slow as mature horses can get without being barred by the veterinarian. I can often see why the crowd singles out one or another horse as the favorite, but I think the reader will profit if he joins me in sitting out these stately processions. Occasionally the winner is something that returns from a layoff after running in maiden-special-weights races. He may be presumed to be stepping down in class. Don't bet on it. His layoff almost certainly was forced by serious illness or injury, and he may not find his winning level until he finally is entered to be claimed for $800 at a county fair.

Increased costs of feeding and training horses have brought us a higher-grade maiden claiming race than was customary in the past. At good tracks, we now have races for maidens entered to be claimed for as much as $40,000. These can be handicapped about as well as a straight maiden or maiden-special event.

48

Regular Claiming Races

At major tracks these races are carded in fifty-seven different varieties, every one of which is worth scrutiny by the player. Careful study sometimes reveals a horse with the class, the consistency, the condition, the style, and the jockey to beat today's particular competition at today's distance. And that's what the reader goes to the track for. As this book progresses, he will get step-by-step procedures for rooting out such horses.

Claiming races are the happiest hunting grounds for smart players. Confined though they are to animals of roughly equal ability and market price, they nevertheless present frequent opportunities for play. Some of the entrants are always without much chance. Some are stale from over-racing. Some are rusty with idleness and are being run into condition to win later. These can be eliminated, because their records proclaim these facts about them. Others are outclassed, attempting to beat better horses than they can be granted much chance of beating. Others are entered at the wrong distance for them, or under jockeys seldom able to do much with them. Some are unable to cope with the kind of pace likely to be set by other horses in the race. Through a process of elimination, the player may find himself crossing out every entrant, thereby pronouncing the race unpredictable and unplayable. But he often will be unable to eliminate one or two horses. The differences between these two will probably be settled by the Plus Factors of handicapping or by a close inspection in the paddock. Claiming races are not only the track's bread and butter, they are the player's as well.

Allowance Races

The conditions under which allowance races are run specify that horses that have won larger or more frequent purses (or both) must carry more weight than will be imposed on entrants with fewer accomplishments. The weight formula is published in the condition book, and the stable knows in advance just what its problem is going to be. Weights are assigned in claiming races by the same method. But the difference, of course, is that a horse entered in an allowance cannot be claimed. Therefore, allowance races attract a better class of horse. A player who goes to the track regularly and reads a racing paper every day is at an advantage in trying to cope with allowance races. Someone who plays the ponies less persistently has extra problems with these events. He cannot be quite sure about the quality of each horse—especially if each has been doing most of its running in allowance races.

The class of allowance races varies widely because the purses do. But the past-performance records do not tell all that must be known. The only way of being dead sure whether the allowance race won by Horse A was better than the $10,000 claimer won by Horse B or the allowance race in which Horse C finished third or the handicap in which Horse D finished fifth, is to have a copy of the condition book, or a collection of results charts. These publications show the size of the purse awarded in every race. The horse that has been running well in races for larger purses can be assumed to be superior to the horse that has been running equally well in races for smaller purses. Sometimes a pace analysis helps the player to penetrate these mysteries without recourse to old results charts or condition books. Indeed, even with condition books or charts, the player is best off when he subjects such a race to the closest and most comprehensive handicapping of which he is capable.

Because allowance races are so varied and attract such a wide range of animals, the only rule that can be propounded in this chapter is the rule of caution. If Horse A seems to be in prime condition and has been running to better pace figures in high-class claiming races than Horse B has been able to muster in allowance and handicap races, what do you do? Do you bet on a claiming horse against a handicap horse? Especially if the handicap horse has been doing much better in his allowance races than the apparently faster claimer has been able to do? If you are a sensible handicapper and can develop no more information than that, you probably pass the race by. High-priced claiming racers often win allowances. But when they lose, it usually is because they are outclassed. The handicapping lore contained in the remainder of this book will help the reader to handle some situations like the one now under discussion, but not all. And if he not only is attentive to what I say but believes what I say, he will pass up any race in which he has to base his bets on wishful thinking rather than informed estimates.

Handicaps

In these races the track's racing secretary assigns weights according to his own handicapping of the entrants' respective chances to win. The horse he regards as best gets the most weight. The horse he regards as worst gets the least. Whereas some of the cheaper races on the card are unplayable because the horses are too poor, most handicaps are unplayable because the horses are too good. The competition is too keen.

Stakes Races

What is true of run-of-the-mill handicap races applies with even greater force to the big stakes races, the highly publicized classics with the huge purses. Secretariat or Ruffian may seem to you to be a standout, a sure thing and, indeed, may be just that. Bet if you must. But don't expect to make substantial amounts of money. When a truly first-rate animal runs, the odds are dreadfully low. And the truly first-rate animals lose just often enough to deprive you of profit.

Hurdles and Steeplechases

These races are thrilling to watch but should not be bet. There are too many ways to lose an ordinary race without putting your money on an animal that has to jump over hedges, fences, and lagoons.

Turf Races

Races run on grass courses are becoming more popular among trainers and owners and are being carded more frequently at major tracks. The trainers like these races because certain sore-footed horses prefer the grass to the dirt and can move up in class by thousands of dollars when their feet don't sting. In general the horse to watch in this kind of contest is the one that has shown a liking for the grass, has a touch of class by comparison with the rest of the pack, and prefers to make his bid in the homestretch after running slightly off the early pace. When such a horse loses, it usually is to a horse that has never run on the grass before but which proves, on first acquaintance, to like the stuff. The safest course for the player is to pass all turf races in which the entire field has not already demonstrated their abilities on grass.

So much for the playable race. To be really playable, of course, it must offer a play—a bettable horse. With frequent and detailed references to the role of the jockey, the upcoming chapters survey the different elements of comprehensive handicapping, the handicapping that turns up the good plays. Here are those elements:

1. *Distance*—I put this first because it is a great labor-saver. If you study a field of horses to see which ones have demonstrated their ability to negotiate today's distance, and if you refuse to give further consideration to horses that either have not gone the distance or have not gone it rapidly, you will reduce most fields by half without even raising a sweat. Moreover, this process rarely eliminates the eventual winner.

2. *Form*—Unless the horse's past-performance record gives positive indications of top physical condition, there is no sense in spending any more time on the animal.

3. *Jockey Assignments and Switches*—If Braulio Baeza rode last time but John Doe is up today, the handicapper had better know what to do about it. The same holds true if John Doe rode last time and Baeza has the mount today. Also, one has to know how to evaluate apprentice jockeys.

4. *Weight*—The importance of this factor is usually exaggerated. On the other hand, a seasoned horse weighted today with substan-

tially more poundage than it has been able to carry in the past is probably overweighted and can be discarded.

5. *Class and Sex*—No factor gives the average horseplayer more trouble than these two. But the problems can be handled, as we shall show.

6. *Consistency*—We have already touched on this in connection with the records of trainers. It becomes even more compelling when the consistency records of the horses themselves are considered.

7. *Pace*—If any horses have survived the foregoing procedures, they are good horses. You now have to differentiate among them. The best method is to judge the probable pace of the race.

8. *Plus Factors*—The separation process is assisted by several dozen of the finer points of handicapping.

9. *The Paddock*—You now have one or two or three contenders left. Until you have seen them in the paddock, you can't be sure what to do. The paddock is where you decide which of the horses, if any, is genuinely fit to do its best.

FOUR / *Know Your Horse*

IN 1950, BILL BOLAND BECAME THE SECOND APPRENTICE JOCKEY ever to ride a Kentucky Derby winner. The horse was Middleground, the trainer was the great Max Hirsch, and the victory was no fluke. Boland was one of the best apprentices of all time. He went on to become an enormously popular and successful journeyman.

A decade after his Derby he began to go out of style. Many trainers decided that he was a bit too much the "sit-still" type to get the most out of a horse, now that so many of the top riders were specialists in whipping and whoop-de-do. It was granted, of course, that Bill Shoemaker was also a sit-still type. And when Baeza came along, it had to be conceded that he, too, was sparing with the whip. This was no help to Boland. Fashion is fashion, in racing as in anything else. Boland was neither a Baeza nor a Shoemaker—or if he was, he did not have the winning statistics to prove it. So he began getting less and less work.

During 1965, when Boland won 102 races and purses which grossed $671,248, it was said more than once that he'd have been nowhere but for Allen Jerkens, the dynamic young trainer who persisted in using him.

"I don't know why Jerkens does it," a daily horseplayer said to me one day. "I can think of a dozen boys who'd get more out of those live horses of his than Boland does. Not that Boland is a bad rider. But he doesn't have that sharp edge anymore. A lot of us think Jerkens would do better with Ussery, Blum, Ycaza, Rotz, Adams, Turcotte, Broussard—or any of at least a dozen other kids around New York."

Much to my delight, this evaluation of Boland was flatly contradicted by one of the game's smartest trainers in a discussion of strong jockeys—riders who hold horses together in the stretch and muster the last drop of speed and spirit for the run to the wire. *"Boland!"* said this trainer. "I wish I could use him more than I do. There's nobody better in a distance race. Forget what you hear. There is no stronger jockey around."

And why couldn't this trainer use Boland as often as he liked?

"Well," the trainer said sheepishly, "you've got to remember that we trainers don't own the horses. The owners do. And a lot of them think that because they are geniuses in their own business they know all about ours. So they act unhappy if we don't have the 'hot' jockeys up. They think that if the leading rider of the meeting or the most popular new apprentice isn't in their colors, they're being short-changed."

On June 4, 1966, Boland won $117,700 for Reginald Webster by riding Amberoid to victory in the Belmont Stakes. The official result chart said, "Amberoid, slow to reach his best stride, steadily improved position after the initial quarter mile, moved out slightly approaching and entering the stretch but took command before reaching the furlong pole and drew clear under brisk urging."

The favorite in the race was Kauai King, winner of the Kentucky Derby and Preakness, but unable to go the one-and-one-half-mile Belmont. Did Boland outride Don Brumfield, Kauai King's jockey? No. Boland had more horse. Kauai King was stale—and possibly aching—from overwork, and showed it by being even more unruly than usual. What he needed was not a race but a rest. So he got still another race—against Buckpasser in the Arlington Classic, and broke down so badly that he had to be retired for keeps. I doubt, however, that he could have gone the distance of the Belmont even if he had been thoroughly fit.

The facts are that there were only three horses in the Belmont with a reasonable chance of winning it. One, of course, was Amberoid. Another was Buffle, which finished a game but thoroughly beaten second under a fine ride by Manuel Ycaza. The third was Advocator, which had been getting some of the purse in race after race and managed once more to finish third. The only time Advocator had won a big race all year was when he was ridden by Eldon Nelson, a paragon of patience. Nelson understood that the horse had only one run in him and needed to be held eight or nine lengths off the pace until the last possible moment—Silky Sullivan style. In the Belmont, however, the capable Johnny Sellers felt unable to let Advocator fall that far back during the early running. Would the horse have come closer to winning if he had expended less energy during the first mile? We'll never know.

What all this analysis adds up to is that a jockey cannot do his best unless he has some horse under him. It also means that the horse cannot do its best unless the jockey manages the journey so as to *get* the best from the animal.

It has long been taken for granted around the big-time tracks that certain jockeys are just naturally best for certain kinds of horses. The long-legged Johnny Sellers and Jim Nichols are thought to bring something extra to the riding of green two-year-olds—although one of the best riders of juveniles in history was Johnny Gilbert, a short-legged fellow. Bill Shoemaker's delicate touch is supposed to provide a bonus in the handling of soft-mouthed fillies. Augie Catalano was a run-of-the-mill reinsman until turf races became popular; for some reason he could ride grass horses like a champ. Heliodoro Gustines has been conceded to be as good as any turf rider of more recent years, although nobody dares suggest that Baeza, Shoemaker, Pincay, Castaneda, and other strong operatives are not good bets against Gustines on the grass, given the right horse.

Let it be agreed, then, that anything less than Bill Boland's superb ride could have defeated Amberoid and won for Buffle in the 1966 Belmont, and that no jockey in the history of the game could have won with Kauai King. Similarly, when the favored Bold Lad finished out of the money in the Suburban Handicap on July 4, 1966, the defeat could not possibly have been the fault of his rider, Braulio Baeza. Most of the fans and many of the horsemen explained the Lad's defeat in terms of the high weight he carried over the one-and-one-quarter miles—135 pounds. Could be. In my opinion, however, he would have been an ill-advised bet if he had been freighted with ten pounds less.

We have now arrived at one of the most important truths in handi-capping, a truth which can save the player untold numbers of losing wagers: *Unless a horse has demonstrated its ability to go today's distance, it should not be bet.* Bold Lad had looked like a champion sprinter, unbeatable at distances up to a mile. To assume that he could carry his brilliant speed even one-sixteenth of a mile farther against good competition was to assume too much. It is all right to *predict* that a horse which has won at six furlongs can win at seven, or that the winner of the one-and-one-quarter Kentucky Derby can go two furlongs farther and win the Belmont. It's all right to predict, because it's fun. But to bet good money on such possibilities is to guarantee long-run losses.

The very basis of successful horseplaying is to bet only on horses *that have shown in the past that they can do what you want them to do today.* When running at longer or shorter distances than they have been able to negotiate successfully in the past, the overwhelm-ing majority of horses are poor bets.

When you find an animal that has proven its ability to run today's distance more rapidly than the ones against which it is entered, and when you notice that it is in condition to repeat this achievement, and when you confirm that the pace of the race is likely to enhance its advantage and that the jockey is the sort able to handle the prob-lem and that the weight is unlikely to spoil things—you have a bet. Otherwise you sit and enjoy the spectacle and let the suckers waste their money.

A really good jockey can usually handle any kind of horse quite well. Especially when he has been on the horse before or has been

57

thoroughly briefed on its idiosyncrasies by a smart trainer. In this connection it pleases me to report that Braulio Baeza is celebrated for paying no attention to the "instructions" he gets from certain trainers, preferring to become acquainted with the horse in his own way—and often winning with animals that other, less-sophisticated jocks are unable to get into the money.

Because of structural defects, injuries, or temperamental quirks, some horses tend to lug in or bear out. A jockey properly forewarned of this kind of thing can sometimes surmount the problem and win (although I seldom bet on it). For example, Kauai King was a notorious lugger. Don Brumfield had to fight him every inch of the way during the Kentucky Derby, and he won it partly because he knew the horse and partly because no other jockey happened to challenge the King for the early lead.

You may have noticed how often the victorious jockey says, "He has a tendency to loaf when he gets the lead, so I shook him up a little at the eighth pole and he kept a-going." The facts are that a majority of Thoroughbreds try to ease up when they get the lead. They don't know anything about clocks. To them everything is hunky-dory if they can't see another horse. A top-notch jockey doesn't permit any such loafing in the stretch, knowing that a loafing horse usually doesn't have time to get back into full stride after something else has passed him.

Front-running horses—specialists in early speed—have a tendency to tire and quit in the stretch. This is different from loafing, but is equally understandable. Energy expended in getting the lead is lost and is not available for the final furlong. Therefore a Laffit Pincay specializes in getting out of the gate in a hurry, taking the lead, and then slowing down—maintaining no more swift a pace than is necessary to stay ahead. This leaves him something to work with in the stretch.

Other quitters (and this is not generally known) are come-from-behind types that lose interest if something else catches them after they have stuck their noses in front. Which is why Pincay, Baeza,

Shoemaker, and others among the more elegant professionals use their whips with vigor when they are on an animal of that type. They know that he is no Exterminator and that they are going to have to encourage him to keep running.

But the skill of the jockey is entirely unavailing if the horse is not entered at an appropriate distance. As the reader becomes a more astute analyst of the past-performance records, he will see that some Thoroughbreds win only for Jockey A, invariably losing under Jockey B. Is this because A is better than B? Not always. More often you find that for this particular horse's trainer, Jockey A is Mr. Right and is given the mount when it is entered at its best distance. Jockey B is Mr. Wrong and rides the animal when it is out for exercise at a longer distance, or shorter.

Nevertheless, most players mishandle the distance factor, and some ignore it altogether. Explaining why, these losers are likely to say, "I leave things like that to the trainer. If he thinks the goat can go today's route, it's good enough for me." They then show you that a horse that had never run farther than six furlongs stole a one-and-one-eighth-miler the other day, leading all the way and paying $28.40. It is impossible to deny such evidence. Sprinters sometimes steal route races. And every now and again a router drops into a sprint and wins it in the last few strides. The number of times such things happen is, of course, infinitesimal in comparison with the number of times sprinters win sprints and routers win routes. I assure the reader that his chances of getting ahead of the ponies will increase sharply when he refuses to bet any horse whose ability at today's precise distance is unclear.

The simplest application of this principle is in two-year-old sprints. Just about the time when the better two-year-olds (the only juveniles worth playing) have sorted themselves out at five furlongs, their races are stretched to five and a half. Before I will bet a *pfennig* on a race over a new distance, I wait for the animals to run it a few times and sort themselves out again. I will consider only one exception in a five-and-a-half furlong race in which none of the entrants has demonstrated absolute superiority at the distance: One sometimes spots a horse that has been gaining large amounts of ground in the stretch while winning (or losing) at five furlongs. If his winning (or losing) races at the shorter distance have been run in faster time than the races of his competitors, and if none of them has shown much life in the final stages of their five-furlong dashes, I may have a bet. The fast-finishing horse may find the new, slightly longer distance comfortable. He may win by five or six lengths, while everything else staggers home pooped. Such things happen every couple of weeks.

When the good two-year-olds are stretched out to six and seven furlongs and, later in the year, to the middle distances of a mile or more, the smart player applies the same criteria. Indeed, when the two-year-olds get beyond six furlongs, I never risk a bet until they've *all* shown what they can do at the new distance.

Handicapping the claiming races for horses aged three and more —the bread-and-butter races—is a bit more complicated. I demand that my candidate's record show something like respectable ability at today's distance. But I do not insist that he have won. He may, for example, have never done better than fourth but may be running against beasts whose own winning efforts were actually mediocre by comparison. Here come my criteria for analysis of the distance factor in claiming races run around one turn. (At most major tracks, this means sprints of up to seven furlongs. At Aqueduct and Arlington Park, the starting gate for races up to a mile is situated in a chute on the backstretch, and the mile races are run very much like sprints—around only one turn.) To qualify for further consideration in a race of this kind, a horse must meet the following standards:

1. *The horse must have finished at least fourth in a claiming race* (*NOT a maiden race*) *at today's distance on a major track.*

During the first half of the calendar year I am more lenient than this with three-year-olds. I will accept any that has managed to finish within two lengths of a winner (regardless of its own finishing position), provided its race was at a higher claiming price than today's. I also accept it—at least for the time being—if it has won a maiden special weights or a maiden claimer of a price at least 25 percent higher than today's claiming price.

The reason for this relative lenience toward three-year-olds is that the more useful ones frequently improve at a great rate during the spring and early summer. All I ask is that the improvement be foreshadowed in the past performances. As to horses aged four or more, I have found that any one of these that has been unable to finish at least fourth at today's distance probably prefers another distance and is a poor risk today. A nag like this surprises me sometimes but not often enough to change my views.

The italicized "major track" is based on the assumption that the reader will be playing his horses at one or another major track. A list appears on page 121. If you frequent a minor track, you can toss out this requirement.

2. *The horse must have run today's exact sprint distance on a fast track on today's circuit, earning a Form speed rating of at least 80, while finishing no more than five-and-a-half lengths behind the winner.*

If today's claiming price is the lowest or next-to-lowest programmed at the particular track, I will accept an animal that has earned a 78 at the distance, provided none of its rivals has done better than 80.

The explanation for this speed requirement (the figures for which are found in the past-performance lines) is that a sprinter unable to run within four seconds or so of the track record in races around only one turn is too sorry a sprinter to merit support at the mutuel windows. As the reader either knows or should hasten to find out, the speed ratings in the *Daily Racing Form* are based on a formula that calls the track record 100 and deducts one point for each fifth of a second by which the horse failed to equal the record. In a six-furlong race won in 1:10, the horse that finished five lengths behind is held to have run five-fifths—or one full second—slower than the winner. His time is calculated as 1:11. If the track record is 1:09, his speed rating for that particular race is given as 90—one point having been deducted for each fifth of a second over the track record.

The reader should note that this speed requirement may be met by a race other than the one which satisfies the earlier requirement of a fourth-place finish.

In case the reader questions my rejection of horses which earn the necessary speed rating while finishing *worse* than five-and-a-half lengths behind the winner, I had better point something out. Chart callers have a devil of a time determining the exact distance behind the winner of anything that finishes farther out of the running than that. A horse that finishes eight lengths back may be credited with doing better—or worse—than he actually did, depending on how busy the chart caller may be at the time. If the player wants to qualify horses that finish six lengths away, there is probably no great harm in it. I simply prefer five and a half.

3. *The race with a speed rating of 80 (or 78) or better on this track or this circuit should have occurred this season.*

Remember, we are talking here about handicapping claiming races. Most horses that run in such races are in something less than prime physical condition to begin with, and tend to become even more decrepit under the stress of too much racing. If a horse has been unable to earn an 80 this year, but did so last year, he may no longer be the horse he was last year. To make sure of this I check his record. If he has been running steadily, without a layoff of much more than a month since his good race at today's distance, he may simply be rounding into form after his journey north from Gulfstream. But if a long layoff shows, the chances are excellent that he went sour and had to be rested. Until he runs another good race, there is no reason to expect that he has another good race in him.

In other words, I will accept a horse off last year's form on this circuit if it has been running steadily. If I find it has been entered recently at the wrong distances, showing early speed while losing longer races, or a nice finishing kick while losing shorter races, I like its presence in today's race all the more, because today's distance is one at which it has performed well in the past.

A problem that arises all the time, but most often during the early weeks of any season, is the horse that has never run today's distance very well on this circuit but shows high speed ratings at other circuits. I recommend that such horses be discarded from consideration. Until they have rounded into condition good enough to meet the modest qualifying rules on *this* circuit, they are seldom serious threats.

Of course, if you happen to be at Suffolk Downs or Atlantic City, and you find that Allen Jerkens has entered something which has not run at this particular track before but has been logging high figures over today's distance at Aqueduct, you had better take the nag seriously. A horse that has been running comparatively rapidly and working out frequently is always a possibility in his first start at a lesser track, especially if he seems in good shape when you look at him in the paddock. What would I do in your place? If I knew for a certainty (from my study of the past performances) that the horse has been coping with better company than he is being asked to face today, and if everything else seems favorable, I might take a flyer on him. But if I were in doubt, I would remember that most horses—in fact an overwhelming majority—never do as well in their first effort at a new track as they will in their second. I therefore would either bet on something else or pass the race entirely. *If the successful player has one all-purpose rule it is: When in Doubt, Pass.*

So much for the distance factor in claiming sprints. If you put it to use, you will discover that you eliminate half or more of the field in many of the races you handicap. This is a great saver of effort. You'll like it. And you will rarely find yourself eliminating the winner. On the occasions when you eliminate the eventual winner, you often will find nothing else to play in the race and will lose nothing. Wait and see!

In analyzing *allowance* and *handicap* races at these sprint distances, I usually cross out anything that has been unable to log an 85. If some of the entrants have run the distance in the 90s, I am ruthless about it.

Races around two turns are handled a bit differently. A claiming horse should not be required to run within four seconds of the track records set by great animals in the distance classics. The 80 requirement is too high. The rule about a fourth-place finish at today's distance remains workable in these middle-distance and route races and should be observed. But speed ratings of 75 or better in claiming races, 69 or better in the cheapest claiming races, and 80 or better in allowances and handicaps, are all that need be asked. Since the speed ratings in cheap route races are often even lower than this, whole fields are eliminated at one fell swoop. I see nothing wrong in that. If a field of horses is too slow, it is too unpredictable.

Races at one-and-one-eighth miles or longer demand more stamina and—among cheaper horses—a little more willingness or class than the sprints and middle-distance races do. Although a horse may seem to be a contender because of a decent speed rating in some recent race, I add a requirement:

To qualify as a contender at one-and-one-eighth miles or longer, the horse must either have won a race of today's distance or must have finished in the money in such a race while gaining ground in the stretch.

Horses that meet all the foregoing standards and that qualify on standards to be set forth later are the horses that give jockeys their chance to affect the winning or losing of races. Because, as I have already pointed out in several ways, unless the jockey is on a horse with a chance to win, *he* has no chance to win. It doesn't matter who he is.

FIVE / *Is It a "Go"?*

THE RACE IS AT SEVEN FURLONGS FOR HORSES ENTERED TO BE claimed for $5,000. The following animals have shown ability at the distance:

A: A $5,000 gelding in excellent condition. Narrowly missed beating slightly better horses five days ago, after staying close to the pace and finishing fast. His regular jockey, up today, is one of the leaders at the meeting. The crowd has made the horse 3 to 1—the second favorite.

B: Three months ago he was beating $6,500 horses and is beginning to regain that good condition. Closed fast in his last race, eight days ago at six furlongs, finishing fourth. Is 4 to 1. Jockey is one of the country's best.

C: An unreliable critter, bothered by intermittent leg trouble. Has beaten the $7,500 kind and recently lost to $4,500 ones but was in the money last week in a race similar to today's. Is 9 to 2. Jockey has won with the horse in the past.

D: The favorite at 5 to 2. A speed horse which led all the way to beat a $5,000 field ten days ago. Hot apprentice up.

E: Another speed horse, led to the stretch call in its last race before running out of gas, and stepping up in class today. Odds are 7 to 1. Good jockey aboard.

Which will win?

Fields of this kind go to the post every day. A good handicapper can sometimes find bets in them. Before he decides to bet, of course, he examines the record of each contending horse much more closely than we have done so far and takes a walk to the paddock to see how the outstanding contenders look. Assuming that the detailed records of the horses running in this particular field contain nothing to contradict the sketchy summaries we have given, the race looks like a toss-up between A and B. D and E figure to tire each other in a duel of early speed, permitting A and B and possibly C to come on in the stretch.

The key to the race is the current condition of B. If he is in anything like top shape, his intrinsic class should outweigh A's competitive sharpness. If, on the other hand, B still needs a race or two before being ready to go after all the marbles, A looks best. Horse A could then lose only if boxed in or forced wide by D, E, and other tiring horses. In such a case, C or B might luck in.

Because A is at his peak, you know that his stable is all out to win. Very likely the boys are betting a wad. But what about B, the key horse in the race? Is it a go? Will the jock shoot the works? Or will the horse be asked for its best only if the sailing is clear? You have noticed, of course, that one of the country's leading riders has the mount on B. He can pick and choose, to get the live ones. Doesn't his presence signify that it's a go? Not necessarily. Perhaps he and the stable want this opportunity for him to familiarize himself with the horse, so that he'll be able to crack down with it more effectively next time out. Maybe he'll urge it strenuously today only if it proves to be in better condition than expected, or if the race turns out easier than expected. Otherwise, he may save the animal for next time, when it can step up into faster company and win at a big mutuel.

No skulduggery is involved here. Assuming that B is not yet ready for its best effort, it would be unreasonable for the stable or the jockey to treat it as if it were. To punish a horse in a probably vain attempt to do the impossible today usually wrecks its chances of doing well next time. You can't get blood out of a turnip, and only fools try.

The reader can probably see by now that the goal of a player confronted with a field of this kind is to discover all he can about the current condition of B. That's what this chapter is about. But before plunging into it, a few words are in order about something else the reader may have noticed: *The best jockeys get the livest mounts, but—as may be the case with B today—they also accept assignments on predictable losers.*

The statistics bear this out. In major-league racing during 1973, only Sandy Hawley, Laffit Pincay, Vince Bracciale, Willie Shoemaker, and Jeff Anderson rode as many as one winner in every five attempts. Boys as capable as Marco Castaneda, Mike Venezia, and Chuck Baltazar, each of whom earned more than $1 million in purses, came in first barely one time out of ten.

Sometimes, we now agree, top boys are up on "no-go" horses— horses that can win only through strokes of luck. But more often than not, the "no-go" ridden by a top jockey will be a "go" one of the next two or three times he gets the assignment, and will win for him somewhere around one in every five or six attempts. If this were not so, the jockey could not maintain his high winning average.

In determining whether today's race is a "go" or not, and what the instructions to the jockey should be, the trainer is concerned with very much the same sort of information that interests the horseplayer. We have already dealt with a key element in his reasoning—the distance factor. And we have suggested that players who underestimate the importance of that factor go to the wars inadequately armed. We also have agreed that the quickest way to reduce a field of horses to its prime contenders is by lopping off the animals that do not actually prefer today's distance.

The next element in handicapping is current condition, or physical fitness, or what horsemen call "form." The cheap horse in sharp form beats his cheap competition because he is in condition to do so. He also beats classier animals whose form is not up to snuff. No aspect of handicapping is more intricate than this effort to decide whether a horse is in form or not. The most frequent reason why two of every three betting favorites lose their races is that the crowd overestimates their current form by comparison with that of the actual winners.

If a horse is properly placed as to distance and class and is in form to run his best, you can be plumb sure that it's a "go." The stable will be trying. The reason they got the animal into shape was to win races with him. If he's in shape, today may be the day. The fact that two or three others in the race are also in winning shape— or that their trainers hope so—complicates matters for the player but does not render his task impossible. Here, as in other aspects of the game, he has a gorgeous advantage over the trainers: He does not have to live with owners. He does not have to succumb to the pressure to get out there and try for purses before everything is 100 percent ipsy-pipsy perfect. He is able (if he tries) to resist the kind of wishful thinking that accounts for so many losses. He can take the over-all view, the long view. He does not have to win races. He only has to win bets. He can confine his wagers to *horses whose records give positive evidence of winning form.* And, glory be, horses of this kind often go off at long odds, having lost their last few races!

In the old days of racing, when it was still something akin to a Sport of Kings, form was even harder to spot than it now is. The past-performance records were sketchier and less reliable. Horses raced less frequently. The best trainers were able—and, for that matter, were expected—to bring a horse into top shape on morning workouts alone, winning race after race from animals whose condition was achieved in actual competition.

Ironically, while the horses suffer and the quality of the sport deteriorates, the wise player benefits from the overactivity to which modern Thoroughbreds are subjected. For every Elliott Burch and Frank Whiteley, who are enabled by the wealth and power of their employers to give all horses in their barns the best possible care, and to race them only when ready, there are at least 3,000 other

68

trainers who run the barns as if they were sausage mills. A Burch or Whiteley animal is a threat to win even if it has not been in a race for months. The same can be said for the horses of few other trainers. It is a rare animal that can be expected to run well today if it has not run in the past few weeks. They don't train them that way no more. And the way they train them, racing them into shape, the smart player can see the blueprint, right before his eyes in the past-performance records.

Here, as in the previous chapter, the operating principle protects the player from the melancholy consequences of wild guessing. To be regarded as in good form, the horse must present *actual evidence* of good form. A study of what the past-performance and workout lines say about form enables the player to lop off as many as two-thirds of whatever horses have survived the earlier study of the distance factor. On occasion, the study of form leaves only a horse or two for additional scrutiny. Not infrequently you will find that the horses suited to today's distance are *all* in less than prime shape. This brands the race as unplayable, because it is unpredictable. You then pass to the next race, your money intact.

The study of form involves two kinds of information:

1. The dates of the horse's recent races and workouts.

2. The kind of performances it has been putting on lately, and the probable effect of these performances on its current condition.

Let's take these categories in order, setting forth useful guidelines.

RECENT ACTION

Most races, including most of the biggest ones, are won by horses that have been active recently. Many handicapping "systems" require the player to discard any animal that has not had a race in five or seven to ten days. Such methods are better than blind stabbing but are only coincidentally related to actual handicapping, which is the exercise of comprehensive knowledge and can never be reduced to the eight or nine rules that comprise most systems.

The fact is that thousands of races are won each year by horses that have not competed in weeks. In my experience at major tracks, however, such horses seldom win *unless thay have something else to recommend them which the player can see for himself in the past-performance records.* Here is how I go about eliminating from further consideration any horse that seems unlikely to be in form to win today's race:

1. *The horse must have had at least one race or at least one work-out in the past twelve calendar days.* To be sure, some horses win at major tracks without recent races or workouts, but it doesn't happen frequently enough to matter. The safe assumption is that a horse that has not raced recently, and for whom workouts are not listed, is an ailing horse. You'll be right ninety-nine times out of a hundred at most tracks.

2. *The horse must show either two races or two workouts, or one of each, within the past seventeen days.*

This does not contradict the previous requirement. It merely adds to it. A total of two workouts in two-and-a-half weeks is not too much to ask. Some experts think I'm altogether too lenient about this. I would agree with them if I did not know that other elements of my handicapping—especially the minutes I spend at the paddock —protect me against horses that are not fit to run.

In *The Compleat Horseplayer* I offered a list of circumstances in which it is possible to waive the two foregoing requirements. The list was rather complicated. To simplify matters, without amending any basic principles or lessening the player's chances of success, I shall now suggest that the player leave the requirements intact except when one of the following circumstances applies:

1. *If the horse's last race was within seven days of today, it need have had no other activity in the past seventeen.*

2. *If the horse is to be ridden today by one of the nation's leading jockeys, or by one of the leading jockeys of the current meeting, it need show only one race or two workouts in the past two-and-a-half weeks.*

The first exception recognizes that a recent race is likely to do as much for a modern horse as a string of workouts. A horse returned to action within a week can be expected to improve.

The second exception is of paramount importance. If one of the country's foremost jockeys accepts a mount properly placed as to distance, it is more than slightly possible that he and the stable regard the undertaking as worthwhile. Rather than discard such a horse prematurely on grounds that it has been insufficiently active, I subject it to further study. It may be a winner, whether it has had two outings in the last seventeen days or not.

To help the reader decide who the country's leading riders are, a list appears on page 86. As to the leading riders of the current meeting, the tabulations in the racing papers and track programs tell you what you need to know. At minor tracks the two or three top names on the daily list, plus (or including) the local hot apprentice or two, can be regarded as the leading riders. At New York and other top tracks, I give the nod to the first four or five riders on the list, and go even further down to include any riders who have been managing to win more than 15 percent of their starts. I also include the leading apprentice or two or three, depending on how many can be regarded as hot.

Modern racing being what it is, the foregoing requirements are insufficient to establish that the average claiming horse has had enough recent action. So here is an additional idea for you to consider:

Regardless of whether it has had a workout within the last twelve days or a total of two within the last seventeen, the horse must have been in an actual race within the past twenty-four.

Any claiming horse that has not run in three or four weeks during warm weather is quite likely to be a suffering horse. I require them to have run in twenty-four days only because twenty-four is halfway between three and four weeks. I apply the same rules to allowance and handicap horses. Here are the exceptions:

1. *Some animals have the ability—or are trained expertly enough —to win at the first asking after a longer layoff.* An allowance horse,

which has been working out at four- or five-day intervals and show-ing a good turn of speed in the process (see page 79), can be conceded the right to rest thirty days between races. A handicap horse can be given even more time—as much as two months for a really top animal whose works have been numerous, recent, and swift. As to a claimer that has not been to the post in the last twenty-four days, I always check its record to see whether any of its vic-tories have come after long rests. If so, I keep it as a contender, at least for the time being.

Some trainers specialize in winning maiden-special-weights events for two-year-olds with horses that have never raced before. Lucien Laurin does it every spring, and Buddy Delp, Dave Vance, Lou Rondinello, Clyde Troutt, and Mike Freeman do it at the drop of a hat, spring and summer. If a first-starter is trained by one of these men and has been working out impressively, I regard it as a con-tender.

You'll have to compile your own list of local trainers who win with first-time starters. It will be tiny. Without it you will not suffer greatly—especially if you have the sense to refrain from betting when you are in doubt. Remember: Most playable races will be claimers for horses aged three and/or older. Much of what you need to know about their current condition will be evident in the dates of their recent races and workouts.

2. *Some horses are consistent performers.* A steed able to win one in every five starts is a paragon of consistency in claiming company. The tabulation in the upper right-hand corner of the past-perfor-mance record gives these statistics. If the horse has had six or more races this year, you can do your arithmetic on this year's record alone. If it has had fewer than six races this year, combine this year's total with last year's and strike an average. A horse that meets these specifications should be regarded as a possible contender in a claiming race even if it has not run for a month. On the other hand, it should show at least three workouts in the past two weeks. Consistent or not, claiming horses suffer from even more severe and

numerous health problems than better horses do. The absence of a consistent claiming racer for a month should arouse suspicion. In retaining him for further scrutiny, we do not abandon suspicion. We merely honor his previous consistency. But we'll be looking closely at him in the paddock.

3. *A horse that scored a "Big Win" in its last outing is discarded if that victory took place more than two weeks ago.* I use the term "Big Win" for the kind of smashing victory that results from absolutely peak form. Such animals are often excellent bets to repeat their triumphs in their next starts, even when moved up in class. Consequently, their trainers like to get them back to the post in a hurry, before the edge is lost. If more than two weeks elapses, you can be suspicious that something has gone wrong. I sometimes accept a claiming animal that comes off a Big Win that took place, say, sixteen days ago, provided it has been working out every four or five days. Maybe—just maybe—the trainer has been unable to find a good spot for it in the meantime. I give a good allowance horse three weeks after a Big Win, and stakes horses get a month.

A Big Win is a race in which the horse reached the stretch call in the lead, or in second position, or, if third, not more than a length or two behind, and then gained in the stretch while winning. The past-performance line might look like this:

$$4 \quad 3 \quad 3^3 \quad 2^2 \quad 2^2 \quad 1^2$$

Readers who do not recognize these numerals as a line from a past-performance record, or are unable to interpret them, should hurry to repair the defect before they attempt to become horse-players. The *Daily Racing Form* publishes full instructions, which merit close study. Meanwhile, let it be agreed that the line says that the horse broke third from Post Position 4, was held slightly off the pace until the stretch, when it poured on the coal and won going away by two lengths. That's a Big Win, and so is *any other race in which the horse set the pace, or ran close to it, and then pulled away at the end.*

We have now disposed of the questions a handicapper should answer for himself about the frequency with which the horses have been getting outdoors. As indicated earlier, this is only part of the study of current condition. The handicapper now must *evaluate* the horse's recent races and decide whether they helped or hindered its condition.

1. *The horse's last race should have been at today's track, at a sister track on the same circuit, or at a nearby track of superior quality.* I pointed out earlier that horses usually do better in their second outing on a new circuit than in the first. Travel takes a toll, and the process of acclimation to new surroundings is seldom an overnight thing. Although an Aqueduct horse dropping into Suffolk Downs or Delaware Park deserves attention and may pose enough of a threat to impel the smart player to pass the race, the Delaware or Suffolk horse invading Aqueduct seldom causes concern. The only ones I worry about are those that were New York horses to begin with and are simply returning home after trying to steal a purse or improve their condition out of town. Similarly, a horse that drops $1,000 or more in claiming price when moving from a lesser to a better circuit might also be viewed with caution, especially if it has been performing frequently or well. As we shall see later, it is foolish to try to handicap horses on their out-of-town form, and the only reason for poring over the record of an invader is to see whether its presence makes today's race unplayable.

2. *The horse must have finished seventh or closer in its last race. If it finished seventh, it must have shown high early speed, or have an alibi for the bad finish.* Every now and then a horse runs an inexcusably dreadful race one week and comes back the following week to win at a $90 mutuel. Such a victory is usually a matter of luck. The horse's jockey sits up there wishing he could get a decent mount once in a while, and all of a sudden the other horses in the race are stalled in a traffic jam and his cripple manages to stagger home by a nose. My point is that a horse that runs a really bad race is usually not in good condition and cannot be relied on for betting

74

purposes until it shows some improvement by running a better race or two. To say that a horse that finishes seventh or worse has run a hopelessly bad race is to be correct, most of the time. On the other hand, the animal that finishes seventh in a twelve-horse field may be in much better shape than the one that finishes sixth in a six-horse field.

Perhaps what I am trying to say is that an animal should not have finished last in its most recent race, and if the field consisted of nine or more horses, it should not have finished worse than seventh. Like all attempts to apply fixed rules to the art of handicapping, this one can cause trouble if applied too mechanically by the literal-minded. I sometimes play horses that finished eighth or ninth in their last starts. And as I just said, a horse may have finished sixth last time without showing a lick of speed, having run against only five other horses.

The reader is urged to use his noodle in this part of the handicapping process. How many horses were in the race? How many did this particular horse manage to beat? How far off the pace was it in the early going? Did it improve its running position, or did it close the gap between itself and the leader at any point during the race? If it seems to have been trailing all the way, or running next to last all the way, without any sign of life, it probably is not ready to go today either.

Folks who need specific rules will find the seventh-place-finish rule workable. Others will profit by looking more closely.

You will notice that I forgive a poor finish if the horse showed high early speed. By this I mean that the horse set the pace in its race, or was close to a reasonably fast pace, before tailing off. The past-performance line might look like this:

$$22\tfrac{1}{5} \quad 45\tfrac{2}{5} \quad 1.11\tfrac{2}{5} \quad 6 \quad 1 \quad 1^3 \quad 1^2 \quad 5^4 \quad 7^8$$

The horse beat everything else out of the gate from Post Position 6 and led for the first half-mile, which was clocked in $45\tfrac{2}{5}$ seconds. It then gave way badly. If it is not the kind of cheap quitter that

75

does this in every one of its races, this recent effort can be looked on as exactly the conditioner needed to hone its running edge. It obviously has been racing and working out frequently, or it would not have survived to this stage of our handicapping. The last race—in which the horse was exercised in the excellent time of 45⅖ seconds for four furlongs—demonstrated that it has its speed. The reason it lost the race was that it was not ready for a winning effort. After getting the rapid half-mile and finding that other horses were still breathing down his neck, the jockey had sense enough not to persevere too violently. He accepted the fact that the horse was tiring and could not hold its lead for the additional quarter mile. To have done anything else would have been to inflict unnecessary punishment, pushing the horse to exhaustion and spoiling its chances today if not ruining them forever.

This kind of seventh-place (or eighth- or ninth-place) finish after a brisk conditioning sprint during the early going is a tip-off to future achievement. Some horseplayers make lists of horses that run that kind of race, and then play them until they win. This is a mistake, because each race is a separate proposition and needs to be handicapped separately. I don't care how promisingly a horse ran in its last race or some other recent start. You can't possibly know what its chances are today until you have examined every other animal in the troop.

Let me now explain what I mean by the kind of "alibi" that excuses a bad finish. Let us say that the horse finished seventh last time out. It did not show high early speed. Before tossing it out, I look at the very end of the past-performance line in the eastern edition of the *Daily Racing Form* for the chartmaker's comment, or "trouble line." If I find that the animal's bad finish was at least partly attributable to racing luck, I call that an alibi and accept the horse for further examination. The line might say "rough trip," "blocked," "forced wide," "impeded," "in close," "disliked slop," "lost whip," or "stumbled." Comments such as these indicate that what happened was not entirely the animal's fault. Sometimes "poor start" is an alibi, suggesting that the jockey was dozing when the bell rang. If the animal always gets away from the post slowly, "poor start" is, of course, no alibi but merely a description of how the varmint normally behaves.

Another kind of alibi derives from the nature of the animal's last race. If it was entered at the wrong distance or in muddy going or against horses of greatly superior class, or was returning to the races after a layoff of more than a month or after a long trip from another circuit, nobody had any good reason to expect it to finish in the money. That's an alibi.

Players who cannot get the *Form*'s eastern edition will be able to judge high early speed from the past-performance line in any other edition but will miss most alibis unless they collect daily results charts, which include detailed comments on the performance of each horse.

3. *The horse must not have bled, run sore, or finished lame in its last race.* This is too obvious for further comment. Watch also for horses that lugged in or bore out. I would not disqualify an animal that lugged in for the first time in its last outing. But if it has done it before, out it goes. Lugging in and bearing out usually result from serious unsoundness. Note, however, that the comment "ran wide" tells nothing about the condition of the horse except that its jock found it necessary or desirable to run far out from the rail. Perhaps he was trying to avoid a melee. Perhaps he had no special hope of winning the race and decided to run briskly on the outside, building the steed's stamina for today.

4. *The horse must not be stepping up in class after a race that it won "driving" while losing ground in the stretch.* Sometimes a horse will get such a big lead that the jockey eases it near the wire and something else gains enough ground to make the winner's past-performance line look as if it had lost ground while expending its best efforts. This kind of thing is not what I have in mind here. If the horse seems to have lost ground in the stretch but the comment is "easily" or "handily," or the horse won by at least two lengths

with the comment "ridden out," the horse is acceptable for now. But the horses I want to discard at this point are those that won in the toughest kind of driving finishes—the ones in which the beast manages to scrape home while something else is gaining. A horse of this sort almost never does well if its next start is against animals even better than those it had such trouble beating last time.

5. *Unless the horse is a three-year-old colt or gelding, it must not have been involved in driving finishes in its last two races.* Three-year-old males can win two, three, four times in succession under the hardest drives. Older horses seldom can take such punishment. The only exceptions I make in claiming races are horses whose last race was a Big Win.

The trouble line often tells whether the finish was a hard drive or not. It will say "hard drive" or "driving" or "game try" or "just missed." The running line will show close competition in the stretch:

$$5 \quad 4 \quad 4^3 \quad 3^1 \quad 2\tfrac{1}{2} \quad 2^{no}$$

Or:

$$3 \quad 1 \quad 1\tfrac{1}{2} \quad 2\tfrac{1}{2} \quad 2\tfrac{1}{2} \quad 1^{hd}$$

6. *If the horse is four or older, its best effort at today's distance must not have occurred in its last race unless the horse is a male and the race was a Big Win.* By its best effort I mean its fastest performance at the distance. Older horses, especially those of the claiming variety, lose their edge in the running of a particularly hard race. If the horse has run today's distance rapidly at out-of-town tracks and you don't know for sure whether the $1:09\tfrac{4}{5}$ race there required as much effort as the 1:10 here, you can simply use the speed rating given to the race by the *Form.*

7. *The horse must not have lost more than two-and-a-half lengths in the stretch during its last race, unless it had an alibi or seemed to be eased up after showing high early speed.* Without an excuse of

some kind, horses that lose ground in the stretch almost always need more racing before achieving peak form.

Anyone who pursues the principles set forth in this chapter will have an extraordinarily good idea of which horses are probably in condition to do their best today. All that remains is the business of discovering the horse whose "best today" is clearly better than that of its competitors. To determine this, the handicapper considers the factors of jockey, weight, class, and pace. He then applies some of the Plus Factors of handicapping, takes his stroll to the paddock, and is ready for action.

Before discussing certain specifics of the jockey factor, a word about workouts is in order. Among claiming horses, the *dates* and *frequency* of the workouts are more important than the times. Animals of that kind are rarely asked for speed except in races. Among better horses, and especially among the better two-year-olds and three-year-olds, the time of the workout is often tremendously important. The only way to know whether a workout is fast or not is to know the average speeds at your particular track. In most places, "even fractions" are considered good—meaning workouts at the rate of twelve seconds per furlong. A breezing workout is more impressive than a handy one. A fast, longer workout is more impressive than a fast, shorter one. A workout from the gate signifies one that is somewhat more swift than a workout from a running start if the times are the same.

In handicapping maiden-special races for two-year-olds, I frequently give the edge to a first-time starter that has been able to work four furlongs in .47 or better or five furlongs in .59 or so at Belmont or Aqueduct. If the youngster is from a good barn and is facing other horses that have shown little in their own races and workouts, it's usually a secure bet.

SIX / *Separating Men from Boys and Winners from Losers*

IN 1915, MACK GARNER LED ALL JOCKEYS WITH 151 VICTORIES, earning purses of $96,628 for his employers. In 1946, with the war over, the game back in full stride, and inflation booming, Ted Atkinson won 233 times and became the first rider ever to account for purses of more than $1 million in a single year. In 1965, Braulio Baeza and Bill Shoemaker each made more than $2 million for racing stables, and eleven other jockeys recorded winnings in excess of $1 million apiece. And in 1973, when Laffit Pincay brought back more than $4 million, eleven other jockeys logged purse earnings in excess of $2 million!

The $500,000 bonuses meted out to a handful of professional football players in annual installments for the duration of their athletic lives are pittances compared with the earnings of successful jockeys. The salary paid to Tom Seaver, the great baseball pitcher, would be a huge cut for Ron Turcotte and would never satisfy Jorge Velasquez or Don Pierce.

On the other hand, dozens of extremely competent jockeys at major tracks earn less money than minor-league infielders do. In no other sport is the disparity between the earnings of superstars and second-flight performers so enormous as in racing. The superstars are simply not that much better. If the capable Ernie Cardone had ridden the same 1,312 horses in 1973 that the capable Walter Blum rode, would he have won 213 of the races and brought back $1,710,461 in purses as Blum did? No knowledgable horseman would bet against it. Yet Cardone, as I mentioned in Chapter Two, is among the scorces of highly competent jockeys who earn less at their trade than is made by millions of machine operators, waiters, mutuel clerks, and chorus girls.

The plight of the unfashionable jockey becomes even more poignantly clear when one considers the travails of Bill Hartack, generally regarded as one of the best race riders of our era. Hartack's problem is that he also is one of the least popular jockeys of our era, having antagonized the press and those who feed racing information to the press. In 1957, Hartack became the first jockey ever to win over $3 million in purses in one year. He also is among the few jockeys ever to tell newspaper reporters, trainers, and owners to drop dead when it seemed to him that they were compromising his integrity, wasting his time, or insulting his intelligence. He has refused to answer silly questions. He has refused to ride horses that he considers unfit to make an honest try. He has demanded repeatedly not to be called "Willie." He has fought City Hall. It happens to be his nature.

In 1957, when he set the record for annual earnings, he rode 1,238 horses, finishing in front 341 times for a winning average of 28. Nobody has ever equaled that winning average when riding so many horses in one year. Bill Shoemaker has come close. But nobody else. Hartack is so good that in 1965, even with his name anathema among the starched bosoms and sycophants of big-time racing, he scrounged 540 mounts and hustled 81 of them home for a winning average of 15 percent.

"Look, I know Hartack is good," explains a trainer. "But owners are funny ducks. Lots of them are in this game for the glamor and the publicity. They want their pictures in the paper. They don't want Hartack on their horses, because they know the press is down on him. The trainers go along with this. Part of the trainer's job is to keep the owner happy. Right? So if the owner is happier with some green apprentice kid on his horse, you put the apprentice on and save yourself trouble."

By definition an apprentice is an inexperienced boy. He is so inexperienced that the rules of racing give his employers extra weight off their horses as an inducement to hire him. It is usually a bum deal. Apprentice riders, including some of the very hottest ones, are usually too green to compete on equal terms with experienced professional riders in race after race. Their records prove it. The leading apprentice of 1973, Steve Valdez, happened to be one of the most precociously talented newcomers of recent years. He won 16 percent of his starts—an average of which any jockey would justifiably be proud. Most other beginners, including several who were idolized as new Tod Sloans and Earle Sandes, won as few as 5 percent.

In New York, New Jersey, Illinois, Maryland, and New England, the season is incomplete that does not feature the exploits of some hot new kid who seems unable to make a wrong move. At this writing, the Maryland–New Jersey hero is Chris McCarron, who won so many races during 1974 that the $2 bettors were nominating him for the Hall of Fame. Whether he would go on to authentic greatness or, like most apprentice whizzes before him, settle into mediocrity as soon as he loses his weight allowance, was a matter of lively discussion.

For an apprentice or a journeyman nothing is more important than a good agent. There are not many, and they are a close-knit bunch. Having to rely as they do on 20 percent or so of the jockey's earnings, they find other sources of income. Some "save" with each other—two or three of them agreeing in advance of a big race to divide the winning agent's share, so that everybody will get a little and insecurity, the element of chance, will be reduced to a comfortable minimum. Some agents run errands for big stables. Some are touts. All are expert students of the condition book. Sad things happen to jockeys who do not have the services of an aggressively influential agent. And good things happen to the boy who catches an agent's eye.

To return to apprentices, hot or otherwise, the player should bear in mind that the hot one usually owes his meteoric rise to the services of an opportunistic agent. The hot kid is, for the period of his hotness, a member of the "in" crowd. He may not be able to ride for beans—if his skills are compared with those of older jocks —but he is not always required to ride well. The mounts he wins on are often the kind that need him only to sit there and whip.

What the trainers like about him—and the reason they fall all over themselves to give him the rides on live horses—is not only that he is on a winning streak and gets a weight allowance; he also is ambitious, eager to please, and entirely fearless, if not downright reckless. That's good. Because he usually has little knowledge of pace, he tries to break quickly from the gate and keep the horse in front as far as it will go. That's not always good. But it happens to be the style in which most races are run and won, whether an apprentice is aboard or not.

One of the things about Steve Valdez and Chris McCarron that intrigued some observers was that they won races run around two turns. In these route races, a boy's patience, judgment of pace, and ability to stay out of switches on the curves make the difference between victory and the Bronx cheer. Apprentices seldom win route races.

Therefore, until the wise player sees ample published evidence to the contrary, he assumes that an apprentice riding in a race around two turns at a major track is going to get licked. The only races in which most apprentices—even most of the hot ones—have an approximately even chance are sprints. And the only kind of sprinter on which they usually hold their own is the kind that gets out there fast. A horse of that kind needs little jockeying. It either sets the pace or stays close to it. It has plenty of room to maneuver. It avoids the traffic hazards encountered by slower-breaking animals.

"One thing about apprentices in cheaper races," says a trainer friend, "they take them more seriously than the big-shot jockeys do. They take more chances. They listen carefully to your instructions and do the best they can to do what you tell them. But a big rider

83

looks on a cheap claiming race as a routine chore. He doesn't knock himself out. He may miss chances that the younger kid will take advantage of. In a big race, of course, the apprentice is no match for the seasoned boy. The experienced rider smells that important dough and settles down to go get it. The apprentice is liable to get all excited and ride even greener than usual. That's why you hardly ever see an apprentice riding in a stakes race, much less winning one."

I shall outline a method of deciding whether a horse that has survived your distance and form analyses is being ridden by a jockey who will probably help his chances. The method helps in another way. It induces you to discard a horse whose jockey assignment suggests that the stable is unwilling or unable to make an all-out attempt to win today. This unwillingness or inability is due in almost every case to the trainer's belief that the horse is not yet in peak shape or that it is "in tough" (matched against too many horses of better quality). A damn-the-torpedoes effort to win with a horse that is "in tough" might blunt the animal's edge without earning a dime of purse money. In these circumstances the average stable doesn't kill itself to get a winning jock.

The principle I follow holds up year after year. It derives from the certainty that a trainer who has taken the pains to get a horse ready for a victory at a first-rate track will leave nothing to chance if he can help it. He will get the best jockey he can find. And because first-rate tracks are cluttered with good jockeys, all of whom crave their 10 percent share of winning purses, the man with a live horse can get a live jock. If the boy is not a consistent winner, the presumption is that the horse is not likely to do much today.

I have already defined consistent horses and consistent trainers in terms of a 20 percent winning average. The same can be said of jockeys although I am inclined to be somewhat more lenient. Because they all have to ride a certain number of stiffs, and because the intrinsic ability of a national champion is not measurably greater than that of, shall I say, a John Ruane or Eddie Maple,

I operate on the theory that the following kinds of jockeys are acceptable:

1. *Any jockey, regardless of reputation or record, who has won with the horse in the past.*

2. *Any jockey who rates among the nation's leaders with respect to percentage of starts won during the previous year.*

3. *Any jockey who rates among the nation's leaders with respect to money won during the previous year.*

4. *Any jockey who either ranks among the top winners at the current meeting or, ranking lower, has a winning average of at least 16 percent.*

5. *The hot apprentice of the current meeting, or any other apprentice listed among its leading riders, provided (a) the horse is a front-runner and the race is to be run around only one turn, or (b) the boy has shown that he can win races around two turns on come-from-behind horses.*

These recommendations mean that if the jockey has not previously won with the horse or is not one of the most successful riders in the business, the horse gets thrown out. Does this make sense? It surely does. Of 2,088 races run at Aqueduct, Belmont Park, and Saratoga during 1973, more than half were won by Pincay, Turcotte, Cordero, Velasquez, Vasquez, Eddie Maple, Venezia, Castaneda, and Baeza. Nine jockeys! Nine jockeys—fewer than 20 percent of all—won more than 50 percent of the races! Another forty jockeys or more won only a minority of the races! If you have a statistician in the family, let him explain what this means in terms of the relative winning chances of one of the more than forty lesser jockeys when pitted against a live horse ridden by one of the top ten. The differences are immense. I am quite sure that similar conditions prevail on every other major circuit.

Am I seriously suggesting that the best-looking horse in the race should be eliminated from consideration if its jockey has never won with it in the past and is not a hot apprentice or a leading rider? I certainly am, especially if the reader is a casual fan. More-experi-

85

enced players can make exceptions as they see fit. Obviously, they will do so without my permission anyhow. An exception I would make any time would be to bet an Anthony Black or a Robyn Smith on the rare occasion when one of them gets a truly live mount. With either of them up, I know for sure that the horse will get a competent, spirited ride.

What about the horse that was piloted last time out by Baeza or Pincay and is to be ridden today by a boy who is reasonably popular but doesn't happen to qualify under any of the criteria listed above? Throw him out. Throw him out even faster than usual. A trainer who was able to get a top rider for his horse last time should be able to get the same rider, or another top one, this time. The fact that he did not is a pretty reliable indication that it is "no go" today.

Remember, most of the races you will be playing will be run by seasoned horses. The jock that won with your horse in the past may not be a leading rider here or anywhere else. But he can win with this horse, and you accept him. You also accept a leading rider, a consistent winner. Why, then, should you accept a chronically unsuccessful rider or an unfashionable rider who has never won with the horse? To do so is to think more wishfully than is profitable in this sport.

Here now is a list of jockeys who earned enough money in bigtime racing during 1973 to inspire confidence—especially when they ride in handicaps, stakes, allowances, or other featured races at major tracks. You can keep the list up to date by using successive editions of *The American Racing Manual*. Note these names well:

Pincay, Ron Turcotte, Velasquez, Cordero, Pierce, Vasquez, Bracciale, Baeza, Maple, Valdez, Hawley, Shoemaker, Alvaro, Pineda, Blum, Fernando Toro, Marco Castaneda, Carlos Barrera, Angel Santiago, John Lively, Mike Hole, Mike Venezia, Don Brumfield, Baltazar, and George Cusimano.

And here is a list of the boys who won 16 percent or more of at least 350 races each on major tracks during 1973. These are the ones who give your horse a bit of an edge in claiming races. These, and whoever happen to be the leading riders at your meeting, are the ones to watch:

Hawley (26.8 percent), Pincay (24.2), Larry Snyder (21.7), Anderson (21.6), Bracciale (20.9), Darrell McHargue (18.7), Cordero (18.5), Avelino Gomez (17.9), Tommy Barrow (16.9), Lou Spindler (16.6), and Blum (16.2).

The New York Racing Commission's annual report does the Aqueduct-Saratoga player the great service of informing him how the jockeys performed when riding favorites. This is extremely worthwhile information for a player who happens to like the favorite. If the jockey is one who wins significantly more races with favorites than other jockeys do, the bet becomes a little safer. Popular jockeys have to be not only popular but authentically talented to bring home favorites at the rate of one in every three attempts. The reason is that their very presence on a horse tends to drag down its mutuel price. The suckers run to the windows and make false favorites of Vasquez or Cordero or Blum horses which, on actual merit, should be going off at higher odds. Here is a list of the New York jocks who equaled or exceeded the average of 33 percent winning favorites during 1973:

Robyn Smith (52 percent), Ruane (46), Baltazar (44), Cordero (40), Gustines (39), Turcotte (39), Daryl Montoya (38), Velasquez (38), Bobby Woodhouse (37), Pincay (34), Lee Moon (33).

Before passing from the matter of jockey assignments to other factors which affect a horse's ability to win a race and which therefore improve or lessen the boy's chances of grabbing 10 percent of the purse, it might be a good idea to review the principles set forth on the past few pages.

If today's jockey has won with the horse in the past, he and the horse remain acceptable. If he has never won with the animal, he had better be a top rider, or it is advisable to toss the horse out on its ear. To determine whether the boy is a top rider, consult the lists given in this chapter (which you should update whenever possible) and apply the sensible criteria which appear on page 85 in italic type. If you do this you will give yourself a winning advantage undreamed of by system players, purchasers of tout sheets, readers of horoscopes, stabbers with hatpins, and purchasers of inside information.

We have by no means finished with the relationship of the jockey to the winning or losing of the race. Much more is to come. En route, we have to consider the effects on the horse's chances of weight, class, consistency, sex (the horse's, not the jockey's), pace, and several dozen Plus Factors. We also must inspect the horse in the paddock and find out more than most players know about what takes place there between trainer and jockey.

SEVEN / *Jockeys and the Weights*

RACEHORSES WEIGH HALF A TON, GIVE OR TAKE A HUNDRED pounds. Northern Dancer was a champion at about 900 pounds. Gallant Fox weighed more than 1,100. On any day at any track small horses beat large ones and large ones beat small ones. The 100- or 200-pound differences between them are canceled by more relevant matters such as class, condition, distance, pace, and jockey.

One of the foundation stones of the game is the belief that if two horses are equal in every respect (an unheard-of phenomenon), the one that carries less weight on its back will defeat the one that carries more. From this, it is but a short step to the belief that if horses are *unequal* in any respect, the difference between them can be compensated by putting a few pounds more weight on the better horse and a few pounds less on the inferior one. And so horsemen measure their activities not only in fifths of a second but in pounds.

The animal that loses by a nose while carrying 119 pounds is expected to win by a neck under 117. To get an extra pound or two off a horse, the trainer studies the condition book like a pirate poring over a map, looking for just the right race, the one in which his nag will get that extra little break in the weights. Meanwhile, the trainers of stakes-winning animals appeal to the American Civil Liberties Union and the Society for the Prevention of Cruelty to Animals if the track's racing secretary puts more than 128 pounds on Baby in the big handicap race. And if Jockey Doe weighs in at 118 pounds when his half-ton horse is supposed to carry only 116, his agent joins the trainer in condemning him for the horse's defeat and warning him that unless he swears off food and shapes up, he might as well go buy a pitchfork and find a job mucking out stalls.

Fred Archer, one of the greatest of British jockeys, took his own life when the ordeal of weight-making proved more than he could endure. Innumerable young men whose natural size is 130 pounds or more undermine their physical and mental health trying to be 114-pound jockeys. With the race of man growing larger every year in well-nourished parts of the world like ours, the 95-pound jockey of yore has become all but extinct. Horses of the quality that used to go to the post under 99 or 100 pounds now carry 110. Such horses win no less frequently than in the past and break down no more frequently. But these facts are overlooked in the general dismay over the increasing size of jockeys and the increasing difficulty of getting a horse in really "light." At Aqueduct, where the owners and trainers are accustomed to nothing but the best, races are nevertheless common in which as many as five horses go to the post with one or two or three more pounds than the published weights require.

The theory that a pound of weight will make a significant difference to a 1,000-pound beast of burden is, for me, a bit too lumpy to swallow. I think it high time that all weight assignments were revised upward by four or five pounds. The entire scale of weight allowances should be nudged up. It would help the sport by assuring every horse a ride by a healthy, properly nourished jockey instead of the woozy-headed malnutrition cases who ride so many races these days. As to the pleas by trainers that higher imposts will hasten the physical breakdown of horses, the proper retort is Baloney. Dozens of celebrated horses have broken down in recent years, becoming crippled before they could run in the Derby and other classics. Thousands of less celebrated horses have broken down (some actually drop dead) during the running of claiming races. In every case the ruination is attributable not to a few extra pounds of weight but to weeks and months and years of cruel overwork, stupid training, and negligent doctoring. In short, human failure.

End of sermon. The purpose of this chapter is to place weight assignments in realistic perspective for the horseplayer so that he will know when to be concerned about them and when to forget them. Accordingly, let us return to the trainer and the condition book. He has an allowance or claiming horse and is looking for a spot. The condition book tells him what kinds of animals will be competing in each allowance and claiming race during the next weeks and how much weight his horse will have to carry if entered.

Claiming horses are given reduced imposts if they have not won since a specified date, or have not won two or three times since such a date, or have never won more than a certain number of races, or if the barn is willing to sell them for $500 or $1,000 less than the top claiming price listed in the conditions of the particular race. Allowance animals get weight off if they have won fewer purses of a specified minimum amount than other entrants have.

The opportunity to send his horse postward with from three to ten pounds less weight than is prescribed by the conditions of a claiming or allowance race is what induces the trainer to take a chance on an apprentice jockey. Of course, if the apprentice happens to be on one of the freakish winning streaks in which five or six of them specialize every year, the extra weight allowance strikes the trainer as a bonus.

I have already indicated that most apprentices are hindrances to most horses but that hot apprentices get good mounts and win lots of races during their periods of popularity. What does this tell us about the importance of the weight allowance? What does it suggest about the significance of weight as a factor in the winning and losing of races?

When an apprentice loses his race, one of two explanations is more likely to be correct than anything else that might be said. First explanation: A green rider and five or seven pounds of weight allowance do not often combine to make a winner out of a horse

91

that had little chance to win in any circumstances. Second: A green jockey often spoils the winning chances of a well-placed horse. The extra weight allowance seldom compensates for the poor ride.

What about the apprentice who wins? What do we say then? Not much. The presence in the winner's circle of the horse and its baby-faced pilot are proof positive that the kid was able to get the animal home in front. Obviously, he did not get it home in front because he is a better jockey than any of the veterans against whom he rode. Equally obviously, the five- or seven-pound weight allowance was not always the reason the horse won. In fact, it seldom is the reason. Nope. The reason the horse won was that, on this particular day the factors of distance, form, class, pace, jockey, weight, and if you don't mind, racing luck, *combined* to give it a winning chance. And no matter how many mistakes the kid made en route, he undeniably got there first.

Therefore, weight is but one factor in the outcome of a race, and in at least nine of every ten races, it is a relatively minor factor. Trainers conspire to get three or four pounds off horses that could win with ten pounds more because they are best. Trainers also conspire to get three or four pounds off horses that could not win with ten pounds less because they are not best. So the smart player lets the trainers conspire but keeps his own eye on the total picture.

To expose the emptiness of the belief that tiny differences in weight are crucial to the outcome of horse races, one need only look at what happens in the races that stir up the most fuss among trainers concerned with weight. The moans and groans of trainers before, during, and after the running of major handicap races are, almost always, moans and groans about two or three pounds. As the reader knows, handicap races are run under weights assigned not by the condition book but by the track's professional handicapper. This functionary decides which horse is best at the distance and assigns it top weight. He then gives the others less weight, according to his estimate of their chances. His purpose is to bring the entire field to the finish line in a dead heat. Such a finish has never occurred in the history of racing and never will. It never will because weight is not that important a factor by comparison with the factors of condition, class, and pace. There have been occasional dead heats involving two horses, and New York officials still revel in a triple dead heat which had everybody talking to himself many years ago. But most handicap races are won by comfortable margins. There is always plenty of daylight (is a city block enough daylight for you?) between the winner and those that finish in the rear. The old saw "Weight brings 'em all together" is true only in theory and would be practical only if horses were robots.

To say this is not to deny that a horse that beats $7,500 milers under 115 pounds may be unable to repeat the victory, even when in shape, if he has to run with 126 pounds. Unless he is an exceptionally sturdy animal and quite unlike most $7,500 milers in this regard, the extra weight will slow him just enough in the stretch to open the way for some competitor who could not get near him when he was carrying the lighter burden.

So the good handicapper takes weight into account. Weight cannot be ignored. It has to be studied, just as every other factor has to be studied before an intelligent bet can be made. But the study, as I shall show, frequently results in a decision that, for this race at least, weight will play no vital part. This is a much different approach from one that overlooks weight entirely. And it is an equally far cry from the nit-picking practice of figuring that a horse will slow down by one length in a sprint if it carries four pounds more than it did last time, and will back up by a length with three more pounds in a mile race, and at a mile and a quarter will lose the length with only one more pound. That kind of arithmetic is too mechanical and overlooks too many other fundamentals of horse racing to be reliable.

One of the crucial aspects of weight that is *never* discussed is the effect on the jockey of riding at his lowest possible poundage. Anybody who has ever seen the jockeys return to their quarters after a race has undoubtedly been shocked at how many of them are gray with exhaustion, their eyes as hollow as the eyes of famine victims, their gait unsteady, their voices trembling with fatigue. Riding in a horse race is no picnic at best, but it is a frightful ordeal for a man who has been starving himself. I believe that one of Bill Shoemaker's constant advantages is his diminutive size. He can ride at 103 pounds without straining himself. If his horse is supposed to carry 115 pounds, a well-fed, clear-headed Shoemaker carries a few lead plates in the saddle pad and that's that. But many leading jockeys can make 115 pounds only by wasting themselves through the cruelest starvation. The effect of this wasting process on their reflexes, their frame of mind, and their general fitness is far more important to the outcome of the race than the poundage itself. In fact, whenever a horse entered in a feature race goes to the post with a pound of overweight, I know that the jockey has tried his damndest to take off those last few ounces, has failed, and will be none the better for it. The refusal by some players to bet on any horse carrying more weight than it was originally assigned makes little sense except with regard to the effect on the rider of an effort to make weight.

Another threadbare axiom of racing is that "live weight" is better than "dead weight," live weight being the weight of the jockey, and dead weight being the metal plates that bring the horse's burden up to the required poundage. In theory a horse assigned 115 pounds is best off with a jockey whose normal riding weight is 115 pounds. This means that the horse carries no dead weight except the saddle and saddle pad and bridle and, of course, the horseshoes. If the jockey happens to be a 100-pounder, the horse has to carry 15 pounds of dead weight. This is supposed to be bad. The argument falls flat as soon as one mentions Shoemaker, of course. The horses he rides in big races carry from twelve to as many as thirty pounds of dead weight. But he wins and wins.

"A short-winded jockey is as bad as a short-winded horse," says a trainer I know. The wise player therefore keeps a weather eye peeled for jockeys with weight problems. The track's condition books list all jockeys and their regular riding weights. Every now and then one of them has trouble making the listed poundage, indicating that he has been straying off the reservation or is bothered by other difficulties and is unable to tolerate the rigorous disciplines of weight making. When you spot such an occurrence, it will pay you to be conservative about risking money on the guy. For one thing, weight-conscious trainers will have noticed his difficulty even before you do, and will themselves become leary about giving him live mounts until they see which way his career is headed.

Most players are unable to keep such close tabs on jockeys. But they fare well enough if they merely apply common sense to the question of weight, keeping a sense of proportion about it, remembering that it is merely one of the factors in handicapping and is almost never the crucial one.

Horses differ in their ability to carry weight. Some cheap ones manage to win distance races under imposts of 122 pounds or more. Other cheap ones can't win sprints unless they carry 116 or less. Some allowance racers show much the same variations when running in fast company but can pick up lots of poundage and win claimers. Good handicap horses win under 130 pounds or more, depending on the distance, the quality of the competition, and the weights assigned to the other leading contenders.

Here is how to go about evaluating the weight factor in allowance and claiming races:

1. *Find the horse's best race at today's distance over a fast track on today's circuit. It usually will be the race in which the horse earned the fastest speed rating, although we shall see later that a speed rating of 90 may actually not represent a race as good as one in which the horse got an 87 but set or overcame a faster early pace.* Remember that this good race should have been run this season, unless the suggestions set forth on pages 62–63 permit the use of a race run last year. This race will be used as the horse's key race not only in evaluating today's weight assignment but in judging today's pace, a critical task.

2. *If the horse is carrying no more weight than it did in the key*

95

race, or if it is assigned 115 pounds or less today, it remains a potential contender and the weight problem is disposed of. Horses unable to win under 115 pounds or less are seldom found at major tracks.

3. *If the horse is carrying up to four pounds more today than in its key race, and if today's impost is above 115 pounds, the horse can be accepted provided it has ever won a race at this distance or longer against company of the same or higher class while carrying today's weight. If it has managed to finish within two lengths of a winner while carrying higher weight than it will carry today, it can also be accepted.*

4. *If the horse will carry five or more pounds more than it did in its key race, it can be accepted, provided it meets the requirements of the above paragraph and also has raced within seven days or has had a workout within four.* The horse would not be on your list if it were not well-placed as to distance, form, and jockey. The trainer's confidence in its ability to carry today's extra poundage successfully is demonstrated by his eagerness to enter it after the recent race or recent workout, either of which can be presumed to have improved its condition.

5. *If the horse is assigned 120 pounds or more today and did not carry within two pounds of today's weight in its key race, all the foregoing requirements must be met.* In claiming and allowance company, 120 pounds is a critical point beyond which relatively few horses are able to carry the mail—especially at distances of seven furlongs or longer.

As the reader becomes more familiar with the sport, he will be able to handle the weight study less rigidly than I suggest. There are times when an improving three-year-old can step up in class and win with 122 pounds even if it has never run with more than 118 in the past. There are other times when the player can allow the best horse in the race an extra pound or two, regardless of the rules set forth in this or any other book. However, the casual player and the beginner will be safer if they stick closely to my suggestions.

As to trying to unravel the weight problem in handicap races, I recommend that the reader bear in mind the high quality of these horses and the relatively slight differences among them. As in any other race, form, pace, distance, class, and jockey are all likely to be more important than weight. On the other hand, the horses are all so good and the differences among them are often so slight that more attention must be paid to weight. Especially at longer distances, relative weight shifts can be a key factor. If Horse A carried 118 pounds to a narrow victory at one-and-one-quarter miles against Horse B, who was carrying 126, it will pay to be wary of Horse B when his weight disadvantage is substantially reduced. This kind of thing happens frequently.

EIGHT / *How to Avoid Outclassed Horses*

HORSEPLAYERS ARE FOREVER TALKING ABOUT THOROUGHBRED "class." Most can identify it, but few can explain it. Class, they say, is what enables a good horse to win as it pleases against a lesser horse. An allowance horse's superior class enables it to beat a claiming horse in slower time than the cheaper animal has been running against its own kind. This is true but not very enlightening. It explains nothing. One might as well say that a classy horse wins races because it gets to the finish line first.

Class becomes less of a mystery when discussed in terms of human beings. For example, Braulio Baeza has class. It sticks out all over him. He is better at his trade than most of his competitors. Why? Because he brings to it an ideal combination of physical and temperamental qualities. Let's see what they are.

Baeza's physical condition is invariably superb—but not better than that of many other riders. His dedication is intense, but an attitude of that kind is taken for granted among top-notchers in any walk of life. His nervous reflexes are swift, but certain exercise boys who lack the stomach for actual competition have reflexes no slower. His courage is legendary, but the average apprentice is a daredevil. To define Baeza's class—his superior quality—one has to observe that (a) his skills as a jockey are complete, and (b) his temperament enables him to employ those skills effectively under all circumstances. The going never gets too tough for him or too complicated. His class permits him to convert the most severe challenge into an opportunity, defeating jockeys whose skills are not inferior to his but whose psychological makeup is less ideally suited to the business at hand.

Baeza undoubtedly was born with the capacity to become a great jockey. Through good fortune the experiences of his life have deepened and strengthened that innate talent. I could name other jockeys who started out with equally abundant natural gifts, and so could you. These men should now have class, as Baeza does, but they do not. Various things have happened to them along the way, and the spirit of the champion is no longer in them.

The same kind of thing happens to Thoroughbred horses. At birth each of them is a potential champion—at least on paper. During the first year of life, some fall by the wayside, their bone structure and musculature branding them as unsuited to racing. When early schooling for the races begins, some prove balky or fractious, and the process of having discipline pounded into them robs more than a few of the winning spirit associated with Thoroughbred class. Hoof and leg injuries common to the breed prevent others—which may have the winning spirit—from capitalizing on it, because they no longer can run as swiftly or as far as sounder horses can.

The class of most three-year-olds is fairly well established by midsummer. The majority have become claiming horses, pushed down the scale of class by defects of spirit or limb. An allowance horse has by now demonstrated its inability to get much in stakes races. A couple of years later the allowance horse will probably be running in claiming races, and some animals that were winning $10,000 and $15,000 claiming races at three will be running for $3,500 or $2,000 or may not be running at all. There are exceptions, of course. Some claiming racers blossom into handicap winners at four, usually after falling into the hands of an understanding trainer. Some useful $7,500 five- and six-year-olds ran for $2,500 at three. But the general tendency is downward. The horse starts at the top, finds its own class level lower on the scale, stays there a year or two, and then enters a decline.

In other words, inherent differences in class separate horses before their careers start. Physical and spiritual wear and tear separate them later. The field entered in a $10,000 claiming race is therefore a motley crew. Each is presumably a $10,000 animal, because it is up for sale at that price. In actuality, however, one will be a former allowance winner with bad legs who is able, on the strength of his intrinsic quality, to lick $10,000 platers whenever his aches subside. Another will be a dyed-in-the-wool cheapie who has been doing nicely against $7,500 ones and may have a chance against the better kind he meets today. Another may be a jaded $15,000 item whose trainer is willing to lose him at bargain rates if only he can cash a bet and collect a purse this afternoon.

One of the things the player desperately needs to know before attempting to predict the outcome of a race is the approximate class of any entrant that is well placed as to distance, weight, and jockey and seems to be in good form. It can be taken for granted that when all other things are reasonably equal, the animal with a bit of class will pull rank on one of less class and whip him. Just as a man of superior quality can draw on his resources to outdo a man of lesser quality, the fit horse with the touch of superior class can turn on the speed when the jockey asks and can hold it long enough to *outclass* the lesser beast. The lesser one may be able to win races in time as fast or faster than the classier animal has been winning his. But today the classier one seems literally to intimidate the other, coming up with just enough foot to get the job done.

Later we shall see how class reflects itself in pace. We also shall see how to assign actual class ratings to horses, enabling the player to employ simple arithmetic in separating contenders. And we shall show, in Chapter 12, on Plus Factors, that certain edges in class make outstanding bets of some horses. At present, however, we are at the stage of handicapping in which we use class as a negative factor, eliminating from further consideration any horse which seems to be at a serious disadvantage in that department.

100

Because we have been going into detail, giving an entire chapter to each main group of handicapping factors, the reader may be wondering whether handicapping is not really too much of a rigamarole to be worth the trouble. He is urged not to lose heart. At the end of the book, everything will be summarized in check-list fashion. Using that summary, and calling on the background supplied by the more detailed material from which the summary derives, he will be able to handicap any playable race in a few minutes.

Here are some guidelines that will help the player to avoid losing bets on animals running out of their class:

1. *No horse aged four or older is acceptable in a handicap or stakes race unless it usually runs in such company and either has won or finished in the money when so entered.* A claiming horse steps up and wins a handicap at a Florida track at least once a season, paying an astronomical mutuel. It even happens in New York once in a while. But it happens so seldom that nobody in possession of his senses will bet on it. As pointed out earlier, most horses have found their levels by age four. The only circumstances in which I even begin to consider the possibility that a cheap four-year-old might win a handicap is when every other horse in the race has an equally dismal record.

2. *A three-year-old whose last outing was a Big Win in allowance company can be accepted in a handicap—but not a stakes race—for three-year-olds but NOT for three-year-olds and older.* Stakes races attract a quality of horses far superior to the kind found in allowance races. Naturally, if the horse in question has been winning or running close in stakes races, he should not be disqualified simply because his last effort happened to be a preparatory gallop in allowance company. The point here is that an allowance horse cannot be expected suddenly to blossom into a stakes winner. As to eliminating three-year-old allowance winners from consideration when they run against *older* handicap horses, it should be emphasized that only a top-notch three-year-old can be conceded a chance against older horses of handicap class. Three-year-olds are by and large too immature to compete against older animals, especially at longer dis-

101

tances. No three-year-old can spot a four- or five-year-old age *and* class. In recent seasons, nevertheless, three-year-olds have been winning more than their expected share of top claiming and allowance races from older horses at Aqueduct. In almost every case, the younger horse has had a class advantage.

3. *A two-year-old that has been winning allowance races is acceptable in stakes races. A two-year-old winner of nothing better than a maiden-special race is acceptable in an allowance race but is not acceptable in a stakes race against previous winners of stakes or allowance races at today's distance.*

4. *No horse aged three or more is acceptable in allowance company unless (a) it has done well against such company in the past or (b) none of the other contenders has won an allowance race or finished in the money in a handicap within the past three months.* Exception: A lightly raced animal from a good barn who has earned a superior pace rating (see the next chapter) in a maiden special.

5. *No horse can step up as much as 50 percent in claiming price (comparing the top claiming price mentioned in today's conditions with the claiming price at which the animal was entered last time).* An exception can be made if the horse has won or finished within a half-length of the winner in a race of today's class or higher at a track at least equal in quality to today's. The class of various tracks is given on page 121.

6. *A horse that has won nothing better than a maiden claimer is unacceptable in a race for winners of two races or more.* The exception would be a three-year-old that has run in the money in a straight claiming race of a value equal to or not over $500 lower than today's.

The Sex Factor

Although most horseplayers know enough to be suspicious of a female horse's chances in a race against males, they are rarely able to decide when the filly or mare has enough class to overcome its natural disadvantage in stamina. I have found that the only females worth supporting against males are those with class advantages and superior pace ratings. Unless a glance at the female's record shows that she is *not outclassed,* I eliminate her at the start of my handicapping.

The key to this phase of the work is an ability to evaluate the actual class difference between a straight claimer and a race for females. A filly whose past-performance record shows a recent victory in an "f-10,000" event is usually looked on as equal in class to a $10,000 colt or gelding. This is an error. The winner of an "f-10,000" is highly unlikely to finish in the money in a "Clm 10,000." Male horses can be counted on to defeat females of apparently equal market value.

Many years ago, while brooding about the mysterious and unpredictable results of certain horse races, I realized that some of the surprises could be forestalled by anyone who figured out how to evaluate the past performances of female claiming animals. In due course I decided that comparison between females and males was facilitated by a simple formula: For handicapping purposes, the value of an f-claimer should be figured at 20 percent less than that of a straight claimer of equal price. Thus, an f-5000 is valued at $4,000. An f-6000 is $4,800. A mare that has won an f-8000 is not outclassed if it is running today against $6,000 males. Take it or leave it, but don't knock it until you try it.

Here is how I go about eliminating outclassed female horses:

1. *No female is acceptable against males unless (a) it has beaten males of today's value at today's distance or longer, or (b) its key race was against males of today's value or higher, or (c) the key race was an f-claimer but the top claiming price set forth in today's conditions is at least 20 percent lower than the claiming price for which the female was entered in the key race.* "Key race" is defined on page 95.

2. *A female is seldom acceptable against males if the top claiming price set forth in the conditions of today's race is $500 or more higher than the price for which the female was entered in her last*

outing. If the last race was an f-claimer, reduce the female's entered price in that race by 20 percent before making the comparison. A female can sometimes move up in class if its last effort was a Big Win over males. Other fillies and mares trying this can be tossed out.

3. *No female may step up any amount, against males or females, if it was in a driving finish in its last race and failed to gain ground during the stretch run.* Females have less stamina than males and lose their form more easily after a tough race. They seldom win after stepping up in class from a race in which they did not have a relatively easy time.

4. *No female may step from a claimer to an allowance race or from an allowance to a handicap unless today's race is for females and no other entrant has been able to win a race of today's class.*

The Consistency Factor

An index to the actual, operational, effective class of an animal is its ability to perform with consistent success against its own kind. Of two $5,000 horses, the one that has been able to win five of its last fifteen starts is a more promising specimen than the one that has been out of the money twelve times in succession.

When I was a beginner at this pastime, I became a great fan of the late Robert Saunders Dowst, a first-rate handicapper whose published works advocated sitting on your hands until you spotted a horse with a distinct edge in consistency. Dowst thought that most people overemphasized the importance of current condition. He loved to bet on a genuinely consistent high-priced animal that had not raced for two months, speculating that its honesty would bring it home. His minimum standard of consistency, which is accepted throughout racing, was one victory in every five attempts. Dowst's principles worked more successfully in the thirties and forties than they do now. He used to be able to hit about 40 percent of his bets, and pursuing his ideas, I was able to do about that well myself. But the game has changed, I think. Every day, relatively inconsistent horses come home in front. Moreover, their victories are predictable.

I have found that consistency is a valuable Plus Factor. A consistent horse that qualifies on distance, form, jockey, weight, class, and pace should be given extra credit for its reliability. But a comparatively inconsistent horse should not be eliminated from consideration. The only ones to eliminate are the chronic losers. Here's how:

1. *Any horse is acceptable if it has won at least twice in fourteen or more starts this year or at least once in seven to thirteen starts this year.*

2. *If the horse has had fewer than seven outings this year, the above standards are applied to its total number of races this year and last year combined.*

3. *These requirements are waived in handicapping maiden races and races for two-year-olds. They also are waived for any horse that finished in the money or within a length of the winner last time out, or for any horse that had an alibi.*

4. *The rules also are waived for any horse stepping down at least $1,000 in price to a level at which it has been able to win or finish within a length of a winner at today's distance.*

If any pigs remain on your list of eligible contenders when you come to these consistency requirements, that unusual state of affairs will be taken care of promptly. On the other hand, you will not eliminate formful horses simply because they have failed to win with admirable consistency in the past. You will rely on your pace calculations, the Plus Factors, and your observation of the horses in the paddock to tell you which of the contenders is the best today.

NINE / "He Has a Clock in His Head"

STEVE JUDGE WAS LOOKING FOR A BOY TO EXERCISE ONE OF HIS horses at old Belmont Park. He spotted Conn McCreary, a half-pint who wanted to be a jockey but was getting no mounts. "Conn, how about working this filly for me?" asked Judge. "Half a mile."

"How fast do you want her to go?" answered McCreary.

Judge was amused at the kid's brashness. "About forty-nine and two," he said.

McCreary breezed the filly the four furlongs in exactly 49⅖ seconds.

With Judge's help, McCreary got three mounts at Belmont, won all three races, and went on to become one of the most popular and successful jockeys of his era.

"He had a clock in his head," said his elders, using the praiseful term reserved for jockeys who know exactly how fast a horse is going.

It is a useful skill. A rider able to count off seconds with any accuracy by saying "One thousand and one, one thousand and two" or "one chimpanzee, two chimpanzees, three chimpanzees" can tell how many seconds it is taking his mount to run between the poles that mark each sixteenth of a mile at the track. If he wants to do a quarter-mile in about twenty-four seconds, he adjusts the horse's stride to bring him to each sixteenth pole in six seconds.

Most good exercise boys can do it. Many good jockeys are thought capable of it. But few actually count seconds during a race. Too many other things interfere. For the average jockey, familiarity with the running style of his own horse and an alert awareness of what other horses in the race are doing (or are likely to do) solve the time and pace problems in most races.

One of Nick Wall's fondest memories is the Santa Anita Handicap of 1941: "I was on Bay View, a three-quarter-mile horse trying to go a mile and a quarter in the mud. He came out of the gate about a length and a half in front. I sat there and never asked him to run a yard and he kept going. They were all sitting behind me waiting for him to stop. At the half I let out a notch and clucked to him and made it three lengths. Coming into the stretch he was three-and-a-half in front. He won by a neck."

And he paid $118.40—58 to 1!

Wall had stolen the race. He had done it not by counting off seconds to himself (which would have done him no good) but by husbanding the resources of his front-runner, slowing it down, demanding no more exertion than was necessary to hold the lead. The horse was perishing in the stretch but had enough left to win by a long neck. Obviously, it could not have won if one of the other jockeys had been counting seconds and had noticed how slowly Wall was going.

Bobby Ussery stole the 1963 Lawrence Realization in much the same way on Dean Carl, breaking that longshot on top and holding it together for the entire one-and-five-eighths miles. Ussery, Angel Cordero, Braulio Baeza, and other veteran masters of the craft win many races on pace-setting animals, getting them out of the gate quickly and then snugging them back to hold the lead at the slowest possible speed. This cannot be done, of course, if the early pace is contested by another horse or two. Unless one front-runner has an absolute edge in class and is several fifths of a second faster in terms of potential early foot, he and the other front-runners exhaust each other. A come-from-behind type sometimes overtakes them in the stretch, if not sooner, and goes on to win.

What we are talking about now, of course, is the most important factor in any race—the pace at which it is run. Ability to get the most from his horse under the conditions created by the pace of the race is the mark of the good jockey. Ability to alter the pace to suit the convenience of his own horse (when he has a horse that can do it) is the mark of an outstanding jockey.

Eddie Arcaro, who had a clock in his head, probably stole more races than any other reinsman in history. He used to steal them in more than one way. Naturally, if he had the only front-running horse in the race, he'd try to steal it by getting out there and then reserving as much of the animal's foot as he could, hoping to last to the wire. But he also stole races on horses that preferred to run behind the early pace. If he sensed that the pace was so slow that one or more of the leaders in the early going would probably have enough left to remain vertical at the finish, he knew that his come-from-behinder was in trouble. A come-from-behind horse is always in trouble if the early leader or leaders fail to poop out.

In such circumstances Arcaro simply would bring his horse out of the pack, pass the pacesetters, and then slow the beast down just enough to remain in front—beating the front-runners at their own game. Naturally, he had to have a good deal of horse under him to get away with this. But his extraordinary ability to size up a developing situation and his remarkable sensitivity to the eccentricities of horses enabled him to do what many other jockeys simply could not begin to do.

I hope the reader noticed the remark that "a come-from-behind horse is always in trouble if the early leader or leaders fail to poop out."

This concept—which is absolutely true—is, of course, entirely at variance with the general notion of how horses run. To the naked eye, the come-from-behinder seems to be running more swiftly at the finish than at the beginning of the race. This fast finish is supposed to be what wins for him. And it is—but it is a fast finish only in the relative sense. Except for an occasional freakish horse like Silky Sullivan, or an occasional freakish race in which the horses seem to walk, not run, out of the starting gate, *all races are run more rapidly in the early stages than at the end.* The winner who comes off the pace to stick his nose out front at the wire is running *more slowly* than he did at the beginning of the race. The reason he wins is that the front-runners he beats *are running even more slowly than he is, and much more slowly than they were running earlier.*

This needs to be understood by anyone who hopes to master pace handicapping. I therefore shall repeat some of these fundamental facts and spell them out in greater detail:

1. All races are run more quickly in the early stages than at the finish. The first quarter-mile of the typical race at most tracks is run at a clocking that ranges from below 22 to slightly above 23 seconds. The final quarter-mile, regardless of the distance of the race, is seldom clocked in less than 24⅕ seconds and may take as long as 26. This holds true whether the race is won by something that leads from wire to wire or by a horse that "comes from out of it" to win in the stretch.

2. The objective of the jockey on a front-running horse is to go the first part of the race as slowly as possible so that he can have enough steam left to run the last part as rapidly as possible.

3. A come-from-behind horse runs the first part of the race slightly more slowly than a front-runner does but almost never runs the last part of the race more rapidly than at the beginning. His style, when measured by the clock, tends toward what horsemen call "an even way of going." His great burst of speed in the stretch run is an optical illusion. He is running faster than the horses he overtakes but only because he has more zip left, not having squandered his energy during the first half-mile. But what actually is happening is that the leaders are "coming back to him"—they are failing in the stretch.

4. This being true, the come-from-behind horse is in grave trouble unless the early leaders tire and come back to him. If they set a slow enough early pace to have something left in the stretch, he will not be able to catch them.

5. The only circumstances in which a come-from-behind horse has a good chance are when (a) the early pace is contested by two

or more front-running types that tire each other out and come back to him, or (b) when he has an absolute class advantage that enables him to overcome whatever pace—fast or slow—may be set by any other horse in the race.

6. On the other hand, a front-running horse with an absolute class advantage will be able to set whatever pace is necessary to beat off other front-runners and yet prevent off-pace animals from catching up in the stretch.

Let's now look at some past-performance lines and see what they indicate about pace:

$$22\tfrac{2}{5} \quad 45\tfrac{3}{5} \quad 1.10\tfrac{2}{5} \quad 9 \quad 2 \quad 1^{2} \quad 1^{\frac{1}{4}} \quad 1^{\frac{1}{2}} \quad 1^{no}$$

This horse broke fast from an outside post position, led at the half-mile in $45\tfrac{3}{5}$, and had just enough left to win. If this was his best performance, one has to assume that he will be defeated when he tangles with another pace-setting type able to get the half-mile in 45 or $45\tfrac{1}{5}$. To match strides with such an animal, this one would have to use too much fuel in the early going, and would be exhausted in the stretch.

$$22\tfrac{2}{5} \quad 45\tfrac{1}{5} \quad 1.10\tfrac{3}{5} \quad 4 \quad 4 \quad 4^{3} \quad 4^{1\frac{1}{4}} \quad 2^{1} \quad 1^{2}$$

The prediction has come true. The pace-setting horse that won the race discussed in the foregoing paragraph has met a Tartar— another early-speed type that cooked its goose by going the half in 45 and a tick. The eventual winner, snugged not too far off the pace, was able to come on in the stretch and pass both front-runners.

The off-pace horse that won the above race did so because it was properly placed as to distance, weight, and jockey, was in form to run honestly, and had the class (or ability or whatever you want to call it) to cope with the early pace set by the other horses. A good handicapper probably would have picked this animal to win the race knowing in advance that neither of the pacesetters had much chance of lasting.

Could the horse have lost? It certainly could have. Under a less than expert ride, or with even a bit of bad luck, it might have been boxed in by the backing-up pacesetters. Another come-from-behinder could have won. *Which is why the player is so careful to be sure that today's jockey has won with the horse in the past (proof of ability to handle it) or is a currently successful reinsman who can be relied on to get the most from the animal.*

The next question, of course, is how in blazes anyone is supposed to be able to tell whether a horse can set—or else cope with—whatever early pace is necessary to win today's race.

The procedure is quite simple. It uses numbers for the sake of convenience but is not mathematical. But before describing it and its variations, a word is in order about the difference between *pace* handicapping and *speed* handicapping. If the reader will refer to the past-performance lines on page 110, he will note that one of the races was run in a final time of 1.10⅖ and the other in 1.10⅗. A speed handicapper would assume that the race with the faster final time was the better race—one-fifth of a second better. His speed charts would make it one or five or ten or a hundred points better, depending on how many points he allowed for each fifth of a second of final time.

But a pace handicapper knows that the slower race was the better. The horse won in 1.10⅗ off a half-mile clocking of 45⅕. The other horse won in a tick less time, but the early pace of his winning race had been only 45⅗. Moreover, the powerful way in which the second horse won off the 45⅕ early pace (it was the kind of Big Win described on page 73) suggests that it could win in this kind of company even if the early pace was 45 or 44⅘. To be accepted as a safe bet against this horse, a front-runner would have to show that it can run the six furlongs in no *worse* than 1.10⅗ after an early pace of 45 or swifter. And the field would have to be free of other front-runners able to pickle it by cutting out equally rapid early fractions.

Here is another example—a seven-furlong race. The best recent performances of the two leading contenders are given:

HORSE A

23 45   1.23⅘ 5 2 2^1 2^1 1^1 1^2

HORSE B

23 45⅗ 1.23⅖ 3 5 5^5 4^4 3^2 2^1

The speed handicapper would latch onto Horse B, assuming that weight shifts did not affect his computations sufficiently to promote Horse A. In justification of his mechanical approach to handicapping, the speed handicapper might attempt to discuss "pace." He would point out that the final three furlongs of B's race were far more rapid than the final three of A's. B was gaining ground all the way to the wire. In today's race B could be expected to overtake A in the stretch and beat him by a length. Why should the speed handicapper predict exactly a length? Easy. Every length between a winner and a loser is regarded as the equivalent of a fifth of a second. Every fifth of a second in final time is regarded, therefore, as the equivalent of a length. Horse A won its race in 1.23⅘. B ran second by one length in a race that was won in 1.23⅖. One length behind the winner makes B's time 1.23⅗, which is a fifth of a second—or one length—better than A's.

A pace handicapper would come up with a quite different forecast. He would realize that A has enough of an early speed advantage over B to win quite easily if the two horses are, as represented, the only real contenders in the race. The pace analyst notes that A was able to run the half-mile in 45⅕ (one length behind the leader's time of 45) and yet had enough left in the stretch to pull ahead and draw away. If his only rival today is B, he probably will be able to go the first half-mile in slower time than 45⅕, saving himself for a vigorous stretch drive, if necessary. If B tries to stay close to A in the early going, which would be necessary to give him much chance at the finish, he would be unable to repeat the swift stretch performance he staged in his best race. To get up that much speed in the stretch, he had to dawdle the first half-mile in 46⅗—a full five lengths or one full second behind the leader. At that rate A would have an insurmountable lead and would be able to hold most of it quite comfortably.

We now see that pace analysis sometimes gives the nod to the front-runner, sometimes to the horse that comes from off the pace. The race run in the faster final time may be rated below a race run in slower final time. But not always!

The object, to repeat something said earlier, is to find the horse able to *set or cope with* the fastest pace likely to be run in today's race. *The only animals subjected to such study are those that have survived earlier phases of the handicapping process.* If a horse is running at the wrong distance or under the wrong jockey or with the wrong weight or is not in form, his best previous races are of no interest today, because you can be reasonably sure that he will not run that well today.

For a proper pace analysis, the handicapper needs three figures. Each of these figures is taken from the horse's best race at today's distance on a fast track (see page 95). For races of less than a mile the figures are:

1. The time in which the key race was clocked at the half-mile. Note that this will be the fractional time of the *leader* in that race, and will *not* be the time of the particular horse *unless he happened to be the leader at the half-mile.*

2. The final time of the key race. This will *not* be the time in which the particular horse ran the race unless he happened to win it.

3. The final time of the horse.

If the horse's key race was run in 45 seconds to the half and 1.10 at the finish and if the horse lost by two lengths, the three figures are 45, 1.10, and 1.10⅖.

If today's early pace is likely to be slower than 45 seconds and the horse is the kind that likes to be out in front or very close to the leader, his final time should improve. But speculation of that kind will be unnecessary. The recommended procedure will give the horse a pace rating—a number that will show how it shapes up by comparison with the other contenders. It is agreed, I hope, that pace ratings are taken from races run on this circuit *on days when the track was fast.*

In races of a mile or longer, the fractional figure is the one given in the results charts or the *Daily Racing Form* past-performance records for the time in which the horse's key race was clocked at the three-quarters (six furlongs). The final time of the race and the final time of the horse itself are also used. For example, if the key race was run in 1.11, 1.36, and the horse lost by a length, the figures would be 1.11, 1.36, and 1.36⅕.

There are many ways of assigning numerical values to these pace figures. Let me set forth the key-race figures of three contenders in a six-furlong sprint:

HORSE A:	44⅘	1.09⅗	1.10	(beaten by two lengths)
HORSE B:	45	1.09⅗	1.09⅗	(won)
HORSE C:	44⅗	1.09	1.09⅕	(lost by a length)

One of the easiest ways to assign pace ratings is to use the streamlined gadget known as Ray Taulbot's Reliable Pace Calculator (obtainable from *American Turf Monthly*, 505 Eighth Ave., New York, N.Y., 10018). If the above races had been run at Arlington Park, the plastic slide rule would give Horse A a rating of 883. Horse B would be evaluated at 884, and Horse C would have a comfortable margin at 891. Players who don't care to buy one of these devices can get the same results with slightly more effort, either by using a speed chart or by a process of direct comparison.

The comparison method is a cinch. Give 10 points to the fastest fractional time shown for any contender, and give each other contender 1 point less for each fifth of a second in which its own race failed to equal that fast fractional time. In this case, C would get 10 points for 44⅗, A would get 9, and B 8. The same thing is done with the final times in which the races were run. Again C gets 10, and this time A and B both get 7. Next, the horse's own final times are compared, with C earning 10 points, B 8, and A 6. The final ratings are 30 for C, 23 for B, and 22 for A.

Note that although the numerals are different from those cranked out by the Taulbot Pace Calculator, the differences among the horses are identical. C is still 7 points better than B and 8 points better than A.

Many players prefer to use speed charts, which do some of the simple arithmetic for them. I shall offer one, but with a few warnings. In the first place, the chart I give you will be just as good as, but no better than, any other chart. The only purpose of a chart is to find out how many lengths' difference—and how many points—are represented by the various fractional- and final-time figures used in pace analysis. Some charts allow five points for each fifth of a second; others allow only one. It doesn't matter: The relationships remain the same.

But—and here comes a warning many charts are sold with the claim that they help the player to compare a race run at one track with a race run at another. I urge the reader not to attempt such a feat. Until a horse has demonstrated what it can do at today's track, or—at the very least—on today's circuit, only an extraordinarily well-informed handicapper has a prayer of giving it a useful pace rating. Tracks vary in contour and in the composition of their soil and in the quality of their horses and the competence of their jockeys. They vary too much for the performances on one circuit to be more than a crude indicator of what any horse will do, pace-wise, on another circuit.

Another fallacy about speed charts is that they make it possible for the player to perform the miracle of rating horses off races run at distances other than the distance of today's race. Forget it. No chart can predict how a horse will fare at today's distance until the horse has actually run the distance.

Now that the warnings are out of the way, here are a couple of charts for you. One assists you in rating the half-mile and final-time figures in sprints. The other is for longer races. The first vertical column contains ratings. The second column lists the half-mile figures you use in pace-rating sprint races. The other columns contain final-time figures. In rating a horse off a six-furlong race, you go first to the half-mile column and find the rating for whatever time the race was clocked in at the half-mile. You then move to the six-furlong column and rate the final time of the race plus the horse's final time. Add the three figures and you have the horse's pace rating.

Please notice that I have saved myself some space and have spared you some eyestrain by not bothering with fifths of a second. Times are given only in round figures. If the horse's race was run in 1.11⅖, you simply deduct two points from the rating given for a 1.11 race. If the horse's race was clocked at 46⅗ to the half-mile, you deduct three points from the rating given to a 46-second half-mile.

SPRINTS

	½ MILE FRACTION	5 FURLONGS	5½ FURLONGS	6 FURLONGS	6½ FURLONGS	7 FURLONGS
100	44	57	1.02	1.08	1.14	1.20
95	45	58	1.03	1.09	1.15	1.21
90	46	59	1.04	1.10	1.16	1.22
85	47	1.00	1.05	1.11	1.17	1.23
80	48	1.01	1.06	1.12	1.18	1.24
75	49	1.02	1.07	1.13	1.19	1.25
70	50	1.03	1.08	1.14	1.20	1.26
65	51	1.04	1.09	1.15	1.21	1.27

Unless you are attempting to handicap turtle races, these figures should do handsomely. On the rare occasion when you find a race run more rapidly to the half-mile than 44, all you do is add the number of fifths of a second by which 44 was beaten. If the fractional time was 43⅗, the rating would be 102.

Using this chart, Horse C of the earlier example would get a rating of 286. Horse B would be rated at 279, and Horse A would come out with 278. Once again, C beats B by 7 and A by 8.

116

LONGER RACES

	¾ MILE FRACTION	1 MILE	1 MILE 70 YARDS	1¹⁄₁₆ MILES	1⅛ MILES	1³⁄₁₆ MILES	1¼ MILES
100	1.08	1.33	1.38	1.39	1.46	1.53	1.59
95	1.09	1.34	1.39	1.40	1.47	1.54	2.00
90	1.10	1.35	1.40	1.41	1.48	1.55	2.01
85	1.11	1.36	1.41	1.42	1.49	1.56	2.02
80	1.12	1.37	1.42	1.43	1.50	1.57	2.03
75	1.13	1.38	1.43	1.44	1.51	1.58	2.04
70	1.14	1.39	1.44	1.45	1.52	1.59	2.05
65	1.15	1.40	1.45	1.46	1.53	2.00	2.06
60	1.16	1.41	1.46	1.47	1.54	2.01	2.07
55	1.17	1.42	1.47	1.48	1.55	2.02	2.08
50	1.18	1.43	1.48	1.49	1.56	2.03	2.09

Suppose today's race is being run at Monmouth Park but the key race of one of the animals was run at Garden State? What then? If the other key races to be rated were also at Garden State, you have no problem. Just go ahead and rate them. But if one was a Garden race and another a Monmouth race, you have to make adjustments that will allow for the differences between the tracks. If you are a steady customer on the Jersey circuit, you should know the current differences. Otherwise, you will have to try a little detective work, or abstain entirely.

As might be expected, most horseplayers commit ruinous errors when they attempt to compare races run at different tracks. They usually base their comparisons on the track records for the particular distance. They assume that the track with the faster record is the faster track. They even assume that the number of fifths of a second by which one track record exceeds another is the number of fifths of a second whereby the one track exceeds the other in speed at the distance. For example, the track record for six furlongs at Garden State is 1.08⅘—four-fifths of a second slower than the Monmouth Park record. But Monmouth Park is not necessarily four-fifths of a second faster at that distance at all times or for all kinds of horses.

117

Speed ratings calculated in terms of track records are often misin-
terpreted by persons who do not realize that certain distinctions
need to be made.

During a given season a horse in form might go six furlongs in
1:11 at Garden State, for a *Daily Racing Form* speed rating of 89.
A few weeks later, in substantially the same form, he might go in
1:11⅕ at Monmouth Park for a speed rating of only 84. The conspicuous decline in speed rating would be attributable (a) to the
difference in the track records and (b) the prevailing similarity in
the intrinsic speed of both tracks.

To keep tabs on the actual differences between tracks, a few
supremely dedicated handicappers compute daily speed variants,
logging the times recorded each day by horses of comparable
quality at whatever tracks interest them. They do this not only in
terms of final times but for every quarter-mile of each relevant race.
When attempting to make pace comparisons of recent performances,
they modify the official fractional and final times by as many fifths
of seconds as are indicated by their records. This kind of nit-picking
permits fairly accurate comparison but is more work than the casual
fan is likely to undertake.

Accordingly, I advise against formal pace comparisons of races
run at different tracks. Instead, the player should either avoid the
issue and not bet or should compare the leading contenders in terms
of their racing styles—without splitting fifths of seconds and hoping
to compute winners by arithmetic. For example, after acquiring
even slight familiarity with the racing circuit and its equine popu-
lation, it is usually possible to recognize that two horses are of
approximately equal speed (judged in terms of final time) but of
different racing styles. One is clearly a front-runner, and the other
prefers to come from behind. If these are the two top contenders in
the race, it is not difficult to analyze the chances of each horse in
terms of the way the race is likely to unfold. Will the early-speed
horse have things pretty much his own way in the beginning, or will
other speed horses press him and tire him?

By whatever method you prefer, you have now pace-rated the contenders in the race. One of them may have a distinct edge over the others. His best race may have been run in distinctly better final time, after a much superior early pace. If this pace rating is ten or more points better than that of another contender, you can believe with some confidence that he has the other contender trounced. In races of seven furlongs or less, it is perfectly all right to discard an animal with so inferior a pace rating, unless to do so would leave you with only one horse. The top-rated animal might be scratched, at which point you would want additional handicapping information on the other contenders. In longer races, it is safest to postpone eliminations of this kind until you have rated the class of each contender. The longer the race, the more profound the effects of class and the less important the raw times in which the horses have been running.

Hopelessly outclassed horses were, of course, discarded some time ago. More subtle differences in class have been indicated by the pace ratings. But a fundamental question remains. In this sport, as in any other, it is important to ask, "Who did he lick?" At any distance, but especially at the longer ones, the horse with a somewhat inferior pace rating may actually be the superior horse. And his superiority will become evident in a study of the kinds of horses he has beaten.

The way I evaluate class enables me to credit a horse with his accomplishments on other circuits without stepping into the booby trap of pace-rating such races. In his previous outings on this circuit he may not have attained peak form. Today may be the day, and the class rating earned on another circuit may be high enough to compensate for the slight inferiority of his local pace rating.

To determine an animal's class, I find the best race it has run *at any major track* in the past three months—that is, the race of highest value that it has managed to win, or get some money in.

Nothing tells more about the actual class of a horse race than the track itself. The $5,000 animal at Green Mountain is outclassed by

$5,000 ones at Aqueduct. Anybody who doubts this is advised for his own protection not to bet against it. The number of minor-track horses that win on the big time without taking a large drop in claiming price can be counted on the fingers of one finger. In fact, the difference in quality between minor tracks and major ones is so great that I, and every good handicapper I know, refuse to credit the minor leaguer with anything until he has earned the esteem at a major track.

The best horses run where the most money is. If Southern California offered year-round racing and paid the highest average purses in the country, Aqueduct would become a second-rate oval. As it is, the length of its season is the chief reason New York continues to command the loyalty of more good barns and more good jockeys than California does. Not many eastern stables are willing to uproot themselves for the meetings at Santa Anita and Hollywood, although some eastern barns keep divisions out there. New Yorkers contend, rather fiercely, that the quality of the races at Aqueduct and Belmont Park is far superior to that of Santa Anita and Hollywood. Superior, perhaps, but not by far. To be sure, the quality of the jockeying is generally superior. Johnny Longden, a West Coast idol, never was much of a winner on the Big Apple. Bill Shoemaker has always had far more trouble winning in New York than in California and, I believe, had the longest losing streak of his career while riding at Aqueduct.

Be that as it may, New York horses are at a disadvantage in California until they become acclimated. The same is true of the California horses that invade New York. For that reason, I have found it useful to assume that a $25,000 New York claimer will not be able to whip $25,000 California horses until he has been in the new environment for a while. Accordingly, I do not give him the full $25,000 class rating. I do the same thing with California animals that invade New York.

On the other hand, New York racing is distinctly superior to that of all circuits other than California. A $7,500 New York horse rounding into form at Rockingham Park will not be overrated if you give him a class edge over that lesser track's $8,000 stock.

Here is my rather well-tested opinion of how the various top circuits rate. If your favorite track is not listed, the quality of the horses and/or the average size of the purses are minor league. The majors:

1. *California:* Hollywood, Santa Anita, Del Mar
2. *New York:* Aqueduct, Belmont, Saratoga
3. *Florida:* Hialeah, Gulfstream; *Illinois:* Arlington, Hawthorne; *New Jersey:* Garden State, Monmouth, Atlantic City; *Maryland:* Bowie, Laurel, Pimlico; *Kentucky:* Keeneland, Churchill Downs
4. *Delaware:* Delaware Park
5. *Pennsylvania:* Keystone

In perusing the recent record of a horse to see what he has been able to beat, I work like this:

1. *Find the highest grade race the horse has won at today's distance at a major track during the past ninety days. If the horse has not won at the distance, find a race in which it has finished within half a length of the winner or, if not that, has at least managed to finish second, third, or fourth.*

2. *Adjust the claiming price given in the past-performance record by using the following formula:*

For races run on this circuit, credit the horse with the full amount of the listed claiming price if it won the race or finished within half a length of the winner. Deduct $500 from the price if it finished second more than half a length back. Deduct $1,000 if it finished third more than half a length back. Deduct $1,750 if it finished fourth more than half a length back.

The adjusted figure is divided by 100, for convenience. If the horse rates at $4,000, I call it 40. If $6,750, I make it 68.

If the final rating is above 100 but below 150, I call it 110. If it is 150, I leave it at 150. If it is above 150, I call it 160. This makes sense because the difference between a $15,000 horse and an $18,-

000 or $20,000 horse is quite slight and should, in any case, be reflected in the pace figures.

If the horse has never run in a claiming race or has done well only in an allowance race, I rate it as "Alw" (for allowance) but make a careful notation of the value of any claiming races in which it has run unsuccessfully. I also pay careful heed to the amounts of money and the number of races it has won. A horse also may be rated "Hcp" (for handicap) or "Stk" (for Stakes), and some confidence can be placed in the rating if its earnings are superior to that of horses with less grandiose ratings.

If the horse's best performance of the past three months, judged in terms of the classiest company against which it competed with success, was at another circuit, class rating is more complicated. The class differences between the out-of-town circuit and today's circuit have to be recognized.

The table below shows what adjustments to make if the horse's best race was on another circuit and his claiming price at that time was less than $5,000. Find today's circuit in the first column. Then read across until you find the circuit on which the other race took place. Adjust the claiming price listed in the past-performance record by adding or subtracting, as indicated.

TODAY'S CIRCUIT	N.Y.	CAL.	FLA., MD., ILL., N.J., KY.	DEL.	PA.
N.Y.		−200	−500	−600	−700
Cal.	−200		−500	−600	−700
Fla., Md., Ill., N.J., Ky.	+500	+500		−100	−200
Del.	+600	+600	+100		−100
Pa.	+700	+700	+200	+100	

If the race being used for class-rating purposes was one in which the horse was entered for $5,000 to $8,000, increase the adjustments by $200.

122

If the horse was entered for more than $8,000, increase the adjustments by $500.

If the class of the horse is to be rated off an allowance race run on another circuit, assign the race a value of $500 more than the highest claiming price at which the animal was able to finish in the money on that circuit, and then make the adjustments as if the horse had been running in a claiming race.

If the horse never ran in a claiming race on that out-of-town circuit, find a claiming race in which it *did* run, increase the price by $500, and make adjustments appropriate to the circuit on which the claiming race was run. This kind of thing becomes pretty imprecise, as you can see, and is best avoided. The facts are that, in ninety-nine out of every hundred allowance races you play, the leading contenders will be class-rated off races run on your own circuit. Or else you won't play. When you begin reaching and stretching to rate a possible contender off allowance and handicap races run on other circuits, you risk the hazards of deep water.

One final, highly important note about the class-rating process: *If the horse is to be rated off an f-claimer, remember that the price for which it was entered in that race must be reduced by 20 percent before all other adjustments are made.*

You now have a pace rating and a class rating for each of your contenders. You may be able to eliminate one or two of them:

1. *Discard any horse whose pace and class ratings are each ten points lower than those of another contender.* If doing this would leave you with only one contender, don't do it. Scratches may eliminate the top one, and you'll want a full handicapping of the other.

2. *Discard all female horses whose pace and class ratings are not superior to those of all male contenders.* Again, refrain if only one other horse has survived.

3. *Before August 1, discard all three-year-olds running against older horses unless their pace and class ratings are superior. After August 1, a three-year-old qualifies if its combined pace and class*

ratings add up to a sum greater than the combined pace-class rat-ings of each older contender. Because no horse can improve as dramatically as an improving three-year-old colt or gelding, I make it a practice to give such a horse extra credit for a Big Win. If it is stepping up in class today after a Big Win last time out, I give it a class rating no lower than the lowest claiming price mentioned in the conditions of today's race. If the animal happens to have earned an even higher class rating at some time in the past ninety days, it gets the higher rating, but it never gets a lower one.

4. *Discard all horses aged eight or more unless their pace and class ratings are the highest in their races.*

If no scratches occur, one of the horses on your list of surviving contenders may be so outstanding as to warrant a substantial bet—provided he looks good in the paddock. For example, I regard the following types as virtually automatic bets:

1. *Any horse that* (a) *rates among the top three on pace and on pace plus class, and* (b) *is either the only front-runner among the surviving contenders, or* (c) *has a pace-setting style and customarily runs to the half mile call (in sprints) or the three-quarters (in routes) a fifth of a second or two more quickly than any of the other contenders.* The horse's past-performance record will be full of 1's and 2's at the early calls of its races. It probably is in good shape to run today, or it would have been eliminated long ago. If nothing else in the list of top contenders is a pace-setting type, this horse is probably an excellent bet. The only adverse possibility is that some cheap noncontender may have an equal lick of early speed. Check to make sure. Most often the front-runners among the noncontenders will not have as much early speed as this horse and will give him no trouble.

2. *One of the top three contenders, if it usually runs slightly off the early pace and is racing today against two or more highly pace-rated front-runners.* You get prices with these.

At this stage I usually write off the chances of any horse that lacks good early speed and is breaking from an outside post position in a race around two turns. At most major tracks, such races are the distance races. Unless the slow-breaking animal has vastly superior pace and class figures, it cannot hope to regain the dreadful amount of ground it loses in the early going. The faster-breaking horses with better post positions run away during the few yards to the first turn and save ground all around the turn. But this poor devil not only has to cover more ground from his post position but has to run even faster than usual in the early stages of the race if he does not want to be outdistanced. From an inside post position, he can, of course, save ground and energy.

The remaining contenders are now studied to see if their records contain any of the Plus Factors of handicapping. One of the automatic-bet types mentioned above need not be put through such scrutiny. But others should. In races close enough to present two or three contenders, even after a rigorous analysis of pace and class, the Plus Factors often show the player that one horse will be a far better bet than the others—provided he looks healthy in the paddock.

For the reader's convenience, I shall reserve the list of Plus Factors until the last chapter, where it will appear in its proper sequence in a review of all the other handicapping suggestions contained in this book. Right now, let's see what happens in paddocks.

TEN / *To Bet or Not to Bet*

"I WISH I COULD READ LIPS," SAID THE DOWNCAST PUNTER AT THE paddock rail. "A guy who could read lips could tell what the trainers and jockeys are talking about. He'd know what horse to bet on."

"If it was as easy as that," replied his sorrowful companion, "every deaf-mute in the country would be a millionaire."

How true. Most races contain from two to six horses whose stables think enough of their chances to bet. Everybody can't be right. There can be only one winner per race. Whether he is a lip reader or not, the player is stuck with the job of deciding which horse, if any, is worth a wager.

Which is where we came in.

Paddock conversations between trainers and jockeys are seldom as conspiratorial as most gamblers think. Sometimes the conversations do not even involve racing strategy. If the horse is well placed and the rider is an expert who knows the animal and its rivals, and if the trainer is a real pro, he may simply boost the jockey into the saddle, pat him on the can, and say, "Get back safe."

My favorite trainer-jockey conversation of all time took place years ago in the Hialeah paddock and consisted of a wisecrack by Jimmy Jones, who was then training for Calumet Farms. Having seated Chris Rogers on Top Lea, Jones glanced at the tote board and saw that the horse was 60 to 1. "He can't be that bad," said Jones to the jockey. "It must be you that's sixty to one."

A young trainer who shall not be named here used to think that horse racing was akin to a game of chess. The rider with the perfect strategy was bound to win. Because the trainer believed that he knew more than any rider, he used to type up elaborate pre-race instructions—page after page of orders covering every possible contingency. Inasmuch as most jockeys read nothing but condition books, results charts, past-performance records, and funny papers, the trainer's typed instructions ranked among the most widely unread literature in the history of the turf.

Ordinarily, instructions are less elaborate than that. "Look, kid," says many a trainer to many a jockey in many a paddock, "don't abuse him. I've got a race picked out for him next week." I know of no jockey who resents such advice—unless he has reason to believe that some other boy will get the ride, and the possible win, when the chips are down. Using today's race to sharpen a horse for next time is just another part of the game. I have not the faintest idea what should be done about it, if anything. Naturally, some horseplayers believe that the betting public should be officially notified whenever a jockey is under instructions to spare his mount the punishment of an all-out stretch drive. If it could be enforced, a regulation to that effect would be something of a reform, I suppose, but would leave horseplayers as sullen as ever. The truth is that every jockey in the business has won races in which he went to the post under orders to take it easy on his mount. After all, if daylight opens up ahead and the horse can gallop home under a mild hand ride, no jockey is sap enough to evade the opportunity.

Trainers and jockeys resemble everyone else engaged in the business of racing. They sometimes win when they least expect to, and they often lose after trying their level best to win. Knowing this, the experienced handicapper spends absolutely no time brooding about his inability to read lips. He goes to the paddock not to eavesdrop on the conversations of sure losers but to exploit his own advantages. Chief of these advantages, as I mentioned earlier, is that, unlike jockeys and trainers, the handicapper does not have to compete unless he has a better-than-average chance to win. He goes to the paddock to look at the horses, either to make sure that the animal he likes is genuinely ready to run its race or to see whether two or three closely matched contenders can be separated on grounds of their appearance and behavior. They often can be.

I said that the handicapper goes to the paddock to look at the horses, but I really meant that he goes to see *his* horse or horses. Just as it makes no sense to waste time pace-rating a horse that is running at the wrong distance, or under the wrong weight, or after an over-long period of inactivity, or against horses that severely outclass him, or with the wrong jockey up, it is unnecessary—and even undesirable—to look too closely at noncontenders in the paddock. The closer attention you pay to the horse in which you are interested, the greater the likelihood that you will see what is wrong with him—if anything is wrong with him to begin with.

Something is wrong with most horses, of course. Which is why the phrase coiners of racing use the term "racing sound." A horse described as "racing sound" is an unsound animal that can be brought into spry enough condition to win once in a while. Estimates as to the percentage of horses that qualify as merely "racing sound" hover about 70. If approximately 10 percent of the horses at the average major track are actually sound (which means free of serious disability) and 70 percent are "racing sound" which means disabled but not seriously enough to prevent an occasional good race), then at least one of every five horses is downright unsound. One of every five horses is in such poor shape that it gets purses only through miraculous upsets and is in grave danger of breaking down permanently at any time.

If you can wangle your way into the receiving barn at your track on any afternoon of racing you will notice that most of the horses are standing in tubs of ice while awaiting the call to the paddock. Tubs of ice cost money. In an era when trainers give horses only half the straw they really need for bedding, so that the labor cost of mucking out stalls will be lower, you can be positive that not a dime would be spent on tubs of ice unless the expense were unavoidable. The ice numbs a horse's unsound shins, ankles, and hoofs, lessening pain and improving whatever chances the sufferer has of running freely that afternoon.

Remember, my experience is confined to major tracks. When I speak of tubs of ice in receiving barns, I am not feeding you my recollections of Upside Downs, where the $800 claiming races are run. I am talking about what happens at Aqueduct, Saratoga, Monmouth Park, and other good tracks. A horse that has to stand in ice before his race is, at best, "racing sound." When free of disabling pain, he may—and sometimes does—have enough class to beat certain animals who need no pre-race refrigeration but have other defects.

Your purpose at the paddock rail is to recognize soreness, lameness, temperamental unreadiness, and staleness—conditions that indicate that the wear and tear of racing have harmed your horse so seriously as to render him unfit for today's competition.

Mind you, lame and sore horses win every day. So do horses so frightened by the sights, sounds, and smells of the track or so reluctant to undergo the torture of racing that they work themselves into a lather of nervous sweat. But horses of that kind are not good bets. To bet on them is to incur extra risks. Betting risks are large enough in the best of circumstances. Who needs extra risks?

A fit and ready horse may show signs of tension during his walk from the receiving barn to the paddock stall. His ears may flick a lot. He may dance, as if on his toes, and toss his head about. But he will not get into a serious battle of muscle and wits with his groom. His coat will have a fine bloom, a deep, dappled gloss that comes from hearty feeding, uncomplicated rest, proper exercise, good circulation, and decent care. He probably will wear the thick "standing bandages" that signifies a stable's willingness to spend a little time and money to protect his legs against accidental injury in

129

the stall. He will not be notably "high in flesh" (fat) in comparison with the other animals in the race.

If he is an inexperienced two-year-old, you can forgive him a pronounced degree of nervousness. He is not yet as accustomed to the commotion of the track as he will be in later months. The chances are that many of his chief rivals in the race are at least equally nervous. Obviously, if the two-year-old with the fastest past performances is relatively calm, you are glad to see it. And if the first-time starter with the clock-cracking workout figures is not only calm but has the short body and wide rump of the born sprinter, you like that too. One thing is for sure: You will find few cripples and no race-weary animals in high-class races for two-year-olds. The only contenders you are likely to rule out in the paddock are those so skittish that they go into panic and expend their racing energy before they get to the post.

An unruly older horse is another proposition. If you watch closely, you will see pitched battles between such a horse and its groom before the saddle has even been put on. The battle often intensifies afterward. Unless you know for a certainty that the horse is the kind of freak that goes on to win after a paddock performance of this kind, you can safely rule it out of consideration. Older horses become unruly when they don't feel up to running. They are jaded with overwork, frenzied with pain. Although horses rank low on the scale of animal intelligence, they associate the receiving barn and the walk to the paddock and the rituals in the saddling enclosure with previous unhappiness and discomfort. They react accordingly.

To be sure, certain national champions have been hard to handle before their races—an argument that has been used against my practice of refusing to bet on seriously fractious horses. But to me there is a tremendous difference between the fractious champion—the "prima donna," and the fractious claiming racer—the pain-afflicted "nobody." The champion is *treated like a champion.* His groom is a man who has been chosen, often at extra expense, because of his ability to handle the particular animal. Such a groom is paid to suffer grievous annoyance from the horse without inflicting harm of his own. If he were to treat the horse roughly, he'd lose his job so fast that his head would swim. He calms the beast. By the time it gets to the post, it is in shape to run like the champ it is.

A fractious claimer is seldom treated with such consideration. In the first place, it is reluctant to run. It is reluctant to run because it is not ready to run. Or vice versa. The stable knows it. The groom knows it. The groom behaves accordingly. The bridle may be equipped with a chain or cord that passes beneath the horse's upper lip, rasping its sensitive gums and pacifying it in much the same way that a knife quiets a human being if held to his jugular vein. Lip cord or no, the horse may kick up its heels and resist the walk to the paddock stall. If the groom responds by snatching the beast's head around, calling it names, using his fists, and generally behaving like a loser, you can be positive that the horse itself is a loser. If the groom knew that the animal had a chance he would do everything he could to ensure the victory, cash the bet, and earn the stable bonus. Stupid as he is, the most stupid groom is aware that the horse's energies are seriously depleted by struggles in the paddock. Grooms treat winners like winners and losers like losers.

"That guy and I aren't going to get along," one of the nation's foremost trainers said to me one morning at the Belmont training track, watching an exercise boy snatch a two-year-old filly back and forth.

"What the hell's the matter with you?" he called to the rider. "No wonder that damned filly is turning bad, the way you treat her. How do you expect her to learn anything with that kind of handling?"

The rider's face was dark with frustration and rage.

"She won't do nothin'," he complained.

"Won't do nothin'!" growled the trainer, thoroughly disgusted. "Hundreds of young horses are ruined by bad treatment," he said. "But what can I do? There isn't enough good help to go around."

Let's return to the paddock. The horses are brought from their

131

stalls and led around the walking ring. Standing bandages have been removed. After walking around the ring two or three times, the horses will be saddled. The jockeys will mount. Twice more around the ring, and then the walk to the track for the post parade and any pre-race workouts. During these few minutes the player should watch the following:

Reluctance

Whether or not the horse fought its handler on the way to the paddock stall, it may become fractious during its walk around the ring. If it behaves badly enough to incur violence from the groom or the trainer or the jockey or all three, it is a probable loser. Notice whether the horse is "washy." Washiness is a lather of sweat, as if the horse were sudsing. If washiness appears early in the paddock proceedings and does not clear up by the time the animal leaves the paddock, nervousness is probably extreme enough to drain racing energy and guarantee a loss. Kidney sweat—a white foam between the horse's rear legs—is a particularly important sign. Some winners show a spot of it when they enter the paddock, but it goes away. If it gets worse, look out. Don't bet—unless you know that this particular horse always washes out and runs well regardless.

Running Bandages

If a probable contender has large bandages on its front legs, I will not bet on it. Large bandages on the front legs are a sign of tendon trouble—real or imminent. The front legs have little to do with the horse's forward propulsion, which comes from the rear. But the front legs take the pounding. If they are at all weak, they can collapse under that pounding. Horses with bandaged front legs win sometimes but lose more often. If such a horse seems otherwise ready to run, I pass the race rather than risk money on it or against it.

By the way, a distinction should be made between the large ban-

132

dages that signify trouble and the smaller ones ("rundown bandages") that protect the horse's ankles from abrasion. These are a help to the animal that needs them and do not mean unfitness.

Similarly, bandaged rear legs seldom seem to indicate a losing effort. Unless, of course, they are accompanied by unruliness or pronounced sweat or by other signs of disability, with which we shall now deal.

Soreness and Lameness

If a horse is sore on one side, it tries to throw its weight to the other, and the resultant unevenness of its gait is noticeable. If it nods its head to one side, the opposite foreleg is painful. If it drops one of its hips, the opposite rear leg hurts. If its forelegs seem to spread, almost to the point of straddling, and it is so reluctant to walk that its gait becomes mincing or choppy, it has sore knees. I never bet on a horse that displays such symptoms (even if it is otherwise calm, dry, and manageable) unless I know that it has been this badly off in the past but has been able to win anyway. In such a case I may defer my decision until I have seen how it behaves during its pre-race warm-up. Horses occasionally "warm out" of their aches in time to win. Others supposedly don't get free of pain until the heat of actual competition—I can think of several orthopedic cases that win once in a while after limping all the way to the starting gate. But nobody could make a nickel betting on such varmints unless he were the kind of soothsayer who could predict exactly when the miracle was going to take place. If he were that kind of soothsayer, he could make himself a million dollars a month playing the stock market.

Pre-Race Workout

If the horse jogs easily to the post, has looked good in the paddock, and seems much the best in your handicapping analysis, you can bet with confidence. If it looked good in the paddock and the boy gallops it about a half-mile before the race, busting it once or twice with the whip, the chances are he wants it to be on its toes for a fast break from the gate and is simply trying to wake it up.

But if the horse aroused your suspicions in the paddock and you want to find out for a certainty whether it is sore or not, pay attention to its stride when the jockey gallops it before the race. If the stride is short and choppy, the animal is sore. If the stride suddenly lengthens and becomes more fluid, the horse is working out the soreness and may be worth your bet. But this will not happen often.

If the boy runs the horse in short rapid bursts before post time, he is making another kind of effort to work out soreness. Sometimes the brief bursts of speed help. But I'd rather risk my coin on horses whose bursts of speed are reserved for the race itself.

I do not know how many horses Bill Hartack has climbed down from in the paddock or during the warm-up period, refusing to ride after deciding that a creature was unfit. But Hartack has done it several times, annoying the poohbahs of racing no end. As far as I know, no horse rejected by the uncompromising Hartack has ever gone on to win. Yet even if one had, Hartack's reluctance to ride cripples remains sensible. A jockey can get killed when a cripple collapses. And bettors lose millions of dollars a year in innocent bets on unfit horses.

In response to such assertions as these, it is possible, of course, to cite cases in which jockeys have refused to ride horses that proceeded to win. One day Bobby Ussery got off Opera Club, a horse trained by Conn McCreary. Angel Cordero accepted the mount and won at a $22 mutuel. Which just goes to show, I admit, that there are no certainties in racing.

ELEVEN / The Running of the Race

THE HORSES APPROACH THE STARTING GATE. THE PLAYER'S WORK is done. He has given a good half-hour of his time to this race. At least twenty minutes were consumed in analyzing distance, form, class, weight, jockey, and pace and in checking the top contenders' records against a list of Plus Factors (which appears in the next chapter). A purposeful ten minutes were spent at the paddock, examining the leading contender. The bet has been made.

And now the variable relationship of the jockey to the winning or losing of a race becomes operative. Sometimes the effect of the jockey is so obscure and subtle that nobody—including the trainer and the jockey himself—ever realizes what actually happens. I am thinking, for example, of how one singularly stupid jockey managed to lose an important stakes race before he even left the dressing room to get on the horse. This dumbbell's mount was a front-runner, a champion, with all the speed in the race, which was being run at a track several hundred miles from the jockey's accustomed haunts. In fact, the jockey had not worked at this particular track for years.

When he arrived at the jockeys' quarters, he accepted the envious comments of the other boys with a gloating smile. He knew he had a shoo-in. They knew it, too. He sat down to savor his good fortune. Along came a lame man selling pencils.

"Wanna buy a pencil? Help an old man? Fer a buck?" said the peddler.

"Get lost," said the big shot. "Can't you see I'm resting?"

This was a mistake.

One of the other jockeys was so browned off at the lofty behavior of the glamor boy from the East that he decided to do something about it. Anybody who not only wouldn't give a buck to a beggar but felt it necessary to upstage the poor old guy was, in this rider's opinion, worthy of special treatment. His own horse was a pretty useful sort with a good turn of speed, the indignant jockey reflected. But it could not hope to keep pace with the champion in the early going without pooping out. Its best chance—an invisibly slim one— was to lay off the pace and hope to catch up in the stretch, counting on someone else to wear out the champ earlier. Not that this seemed possible, the competition being what it was.

The only way to beat the phony from the East was to take his own horse out there right from the start and run as fast as he could, the jockey realized. He'd beat his own horse in the process, but what the hell, he'd wreck that stuck-up big-timer in the bargain. And he didn't figure to win with his own horse anyhow, no matter how he rode.

So he got out of the gate with the big shot and ran him to the fastest half-mile in history (up to that date). The champ was ruined. Both horses finished out of the money, of course. It wouldn't have happened if the champion's jockey had been courteous to the peddler.

The jockey's responsibility for a loss rarely is that flagrant. Even when a green apprentice allows a horse to shoot its bolt in the first half-mile, or runs it into an open switch on the turn, getting hemmed in during the stretch drive, nobody can be positive that the horse would have won under a better ride. All that can be said is that the ride was not good.

Frequently, the difference between a winning and losing ride may be the boy's hesitation for a twentieth of a second—enough hesitation to account for his defeat by a nose. But it all happens so quickly that nobody *knows* it happens. Afterward the jockey says, "I brought him around horses because I couldn't get through on the rail. I thought I had it won until that other horse came alongside. My horse didn't have that one extra jump he needed." And the reason, of course, is that the extra jump was wasted three-eighths of a mile from the finish line. If the jock had been Pincay or Hawley, for whom a twentieth of a second is ample time for decision, he would have gone into the hole on the rail and would have won by a length.

Which illustrates why it pays to stick with jockeys who win more than their share of races, nationally or locally. One reason horses win more often for top riders *is that these riders run into less trouble during their races.* Other jockeys call it luck, or the breaks. But it's usually more than that. It usually is a tiny edge in ability. This small advantage enables the top-notcher to give the best horse in the race the ride it needs to prove its superiority. And sometimes a top-notch rider can use his edge to make a winner of the second- or third-best horse.

Running into switches, missing opportunities through hesitation, misjudging pace, or failing to adapt riding tactics to the infinite variety of unpredictable split-second problems that arise are by no means the only ways jockeys lose races they should win. When competitive zeal becomes so great that it endangers the lives of other jockeys or prevents their mounts from running freely, the rules intervene to punish the zeal. For example, if a jockey brings his horse over to the rail too abruptly, forcing another rider to take back and break stride rather than risk a fatal collision, the guilty jockey will almost certainly be disqualified if he happens to arrive at the finish wire first, second, or third. His infraction may have been careless, rather than intentional, but the rules are strict (especially in New York).

Most jockeys are glad of this. If it weren't for the patrol judges and the official films of the races, injury and death would be even

137

more common today than in the past. Reason? The purses are larger today and the competition for them is keener. A boy who thought he could get away with dangerous tactics would be tempted to take the chance. "It would be a license to kill," one jockey told me.

It used to be just that in the old days. With nobody to penalize roughness, riders used to stay much closer to the adjoining horses than they do now. They would stick their elbows into a rival's reins, press a heel against the other horse's stifle, push the other horse with a hand or foot while it was in the air—knocking it six feet sideways. They would hook a heel into the other jock's stirrup or grab his saddlecloth with a hand, holding him back. "Get out of the way or I'll tear down the infield fence with you," an offended rider would say, and many were the pile-ups on those fences.

New York officials have led the movement toward polite, sportsmanlike riding tactics. They still quake (as well they might) over the appalled and indignant reaction of the public to the deaths of jockeys like Sidney Cole and Roy Gilbert. New York is altogether the Sunday school of Thoroughbred racing. A New York rider must win on merit alone, without resort to rough or unethical tactics. And he has to behave himself off the track. His every move is watched. A certain jockey who made the error of taking a vacation in Las Vegas and associating with known gamblers there is no longer seen on the New York circuit. (Exactly how one could be in Las Vegas *without* associating with known gamblers is, perhaps, beside the point.)

If the patrol judges at Aqueduct are concerned mainly with rough riding, those at Santa Anita, Hollywood, and Del Mar are more interested in spotting unvigorous riding. A California jockey gets in trouble for riding a weak race. He gets in less trouble for interfering with another horse. Indeed, Californians saw absolutely nothing wrong with the tactics Johnny Longden employed in winning the last race of his career, the 1966 San Juan Capistrano Handicap. When Manuel Ycaza tried to move outside on Hill Rise, Longden brought George Royal over, blocking him. Ycaza had to pull back and break stride. In New York, Longden might have been disqualified. In California, his interference attracted only mild comment.

What happened to Ycaza in that race was, of course, a kind of poetic justice. Aside from Ralph "Pepper Pot" Neves and Pete Anderson, Ycaza was the roughest top rider of recent years. A jockey tells me, "Neves could not go by you without bothering you. He was always squeezing, brushing, getting in your way. Ycaza was the same. It wasn't enough to have the best horse, he had to *beat* the other guy. It's all right to want to win, but it costs big dough to be set down for ten days. A rider can make thousands of dollars in ten days. But not if he's suspended."

This is indeed the only game in which one athlete will kill another to win a purse unless the rules prevent it. In boxing, the object of which is to hurt the other man, the participants have a genuine regard for each other. They seldom inflict unnecessary punishment. Before and after the fight, they may be close friends. They do not often permit the heat of combat to annul the friendship. But jockeys, cordial though they are to each other between races, are homicidally competitive. Perhaps the best illustration of this competitive spirit is the story of the great Don Meade, who may have been among the five best riders of all time. Jockeys are supposed to bet only on their own horse, and then only by placing the bet through the horse's owner. But Meade used to bet on horses against which he was racing. After the officials learned of this, they put a tap on his telephone. They caught him betting against himself in twenty-seven races. His license was revoked. An aspect of the tragedy that got little or no publicity was this: All twenty-seven of the illegal bets lost! And Meade, bets to the contrary notwithstanding, finished first on his own mounts in eleven of the twenty-seven races!

A few years ago a friend of mine told about a financial calamity that had befallen him. A well-known jockey had telephoned with a hot tip. The horse would be ridden by another boy, but the tipster would be in the same race, sort of to make sure that nothing went wrong. Result: The hot tip lost, but the jockey's own mount won.

The penalties for unauthorized betting and touting are so severe, and Big Brother is watching so closely, that jockeys are careful to project an image of absolute rectitude. Needless to say, some of them tout anyhow, and make good money at it. Others are slaves to the mutuel machines. But none that I know of makes the mistake of betting against himself, Meade-style.

In trying to understand why a jockey loses on a mount that shaped up in advance as best in its race, many players wax indignant about "fixes." They become so fix-minded that in addition to trying to read lips in the paddock, they watch each jockey closely during the post parade to see if he is sending "signals" to confederates in the crowd. If he waves his whip, it's a signal. If he sneezes, it's a signal. Or if he smiles. Or does not smile. Because they want to avoid suspicion, some jocks attempt to wear absolutely expressionless faces aboard a horse, looking neither left nor right. It is impossible.

The facts are that certain jockeys, including some of the best, have had clandestine "pieces" of racing stables and have been involved in betting manipulations involving tens of thousands of dollars. But, as I have attempted to show, a really good jockey is so good—so *incurably* good—that he can be relied on to put forth a winning effort when he is on a horse capable of it. The rewards for a successful ride are so generous, and the penalties for deliberately dumping a race so severe, that the old-fashioned betting coup, in which three or four riders would conspire to assure victory to one of them, is virtually unheard of nowadays except in wild rumor. The only kinds of coup I know about in modern big-league racing are the sort that the good handicapper can sometimes predict from a careful study of past performances—the crackdown by a good jockey on a horse whose form has been concealed by defeats at the wrong distance or in the wrong company or under the wrong weights.

I understand that jockeys continue to "save" with each other—agreeing in advance to divide the winning rider's share of a large purse. The practice has been outlawed by the rule makers because it

140

smacks of collusion. But it persists, just as it does in professional golf, which has also outlawed it.

Artificial aids to victory like concealed batteries, stimulating or pain-killing drugs, and the like have also been outlawed. But the year seldom passes without some lesser jockey getting caught with a battery. A mild electric shock has a dramatic effect on a horse that tends to quit in the stretch. In trying to run away from the pain, it forgets to quit. Much the same effect is obtained by riders who conceal needle-sharp carpentry nails in their mouths, stabbing their steeds in the mane or neck with the tiny weapons and then spitting them out at the finish line. Hedley Woodhouse did not use nails, as far as I know, but he has gone on record as biting his horses on the neck to keep them together in the stretch. Any day now, racing officialdom can be expected to outlaw teeth. And Carlos Lopez says that the stewards in Puerto Rico inspect the length of each rider's *fingernails!*

With or without nails, or teeth, or batteries, horse racing remains very much like poker or bridge. There is a good deal of luck in it, but ability wins out in the end. Which is why racetrack gamblers, horse trainers, and jockey agents make so little sense when they behave as if a jockey should be able to win races on bad horses. Good jockeys become accustomed to such abuse, but they never become indifferent to it. Once in a while they expose it for the nonsense that it is.

"What's the matter with you?" sputtered a lame-brained trainer at Eddie Arcaro after a losing race. "I told you to lay back until the three-eighth pole and then come on in the stretch!"

To which The Master is supposed to have replied, "I guess I could have done it, but I figured I'd better stay on the horse."

141

TWELVE / *Handicapping*
with Plus Factors

THE RELATIONSHIP OF JOCKEYS TO THE WINNING OR LOSING OF horse races has now been described in considerable depth.

We have surveyed the cliff-hanging economics and cutthroat politics of Thoroughbred racing, showing how the pressures affect everything a trainer does with his horse—from the kind of conditioning he gives it to the kind of jockey he employs.

We have discussed the strategy, the tactics, and the techniques of race riding.

We have shown that successful jockeys are not invariably better riders than less successful jockeys but that successful jockeys usually get the best mounts.

With reference to the official statistics of the game, we have seen why a smart player risks his money only when the right horse has been paired with the right jockey.

We have examined a method of identifying the "right" jockey, as part of an over-all approach to the handicapping of races.

In the course of this presentation, several references have been made to the Plus Factors of handicapping. Readers of *The Compleat Horseplayer* will recall that the book presented forty Plus Factors and demonstrated how these detailed aspects of a horse's past-performance record enable the player to differentiate an outstanding bet from a merely promising one. The list of Plus Factors has been improved by adding some of the statistical discoveries of Frederick S. Davis (see page 7). The list will be set forth in this chapter, after a summary of the handicapping advice contained in earlier chapters.

As before, the various stages of handicapping will be outlined in a sequence which enables the player to discard improperly placed horses quickly and isolate the actual contenders for deeper study.

BASIC PRINCIPLES

The player's objective is to find a horse that not only is well suited to today's distance, class, weight, and jockey but is in condition to do its best. If its best, as shown in the past-performance record, is better than the best of any other logical contender, the horse is a good risk.

TWO-YEAR-OLD RACES

At distances of less than six furlongs, play maiden special weights, allowances, and stakes, favoring any horse that has been running the exact distance in the fastest time. If no horse has been running the distance swiftly (by comparison with the times set in similar races at the track this season), play a first-time starter that has been working out in impressive style. At distances of six furlongs and up, favor the animal with the highest pace rating. Play no maiden-claiming races unless one of the starters has been running in maiden-special-weights events at speeds no worse than those of the horses against which it competes today.

OLDER HORSES

Distance

Eliminate all horses that have shown no real ability at today's exact distance. To qualify in a claiming race, a contender should have finished fourth or better at the distance in a straight claimer

at some major track. Until July a three-year-old can be accepted if
it has run almost that well in a race of higher claiming price than
today's or if it has won a maiden claimer at a price at least 25 percent above today's, or a maiden special.

Either in the aforementioned race or some other at the distance,
the horse must have earned a *Racing Form* speed rating of at least
80 in a sprint or 75 in a route, on a fast track on today's circuit,
finishing no worse than five-and-a-half lengths behind. If today's
top claiming price is $4,000 or less, a horse with a 78 is acceptable
in a sprint provided that no rival shows an 81 or better. In a route
of this low class, 69 is all right. In allowance and handicap races
the player should demand a previous speed rating of 85—sometimes
higher, depending on the general quality of the horses.

The qualifying race (in which the speed rating was earned)
should have taken place this season, unless the horse has been running steadily since last season with no layoffs of more than a month.

In races at one-and-one-eighth-miles or longer, the horse must
either have won at today's exact distance or must have finished in
the money while gaining ground in the stretch.

Form

The horse must have had at least one race or one workout within
the last twelve calendar days.

The horse also must show either two races or two workouts, or
one of each, in the past seventeen days unless its last race was
within seven days. Also, if the horse is to be ridden by one of the
nation's leading jockeys or by one of the leading jockeys of the
current meeting, it need show only *one* race or two workouts in the
past two-and-a-half weeks and the twelve-day requirement is waived
(see pages 70 and 71).

Regardless of the foregoing, the horse must have had an actual
race within the past twenty-four days unless it has won after a long
layoff in the past (allow it thirty days now) or is a consistent animal that has been working out frequently (see pages 71 and 72).

A horse that scored a Big Win in its last race is discarded if that victory occurred more than two weeks ago and the animal has not been working out steadily.

The horse's last race should have been on today's circuit or a nearby track of superior quality unless it is dropping down in class or is returning to its home track after a short trip elsewhere.

The horse must have finished seventh or better (see page 74) in its last race unless it had an alibi or showed high early speed.

The horse must not have bled, run sore, or finished lame in its last race.

The horse must not be stepping up in class after a race that it won "driving" while losing ground in the stretch.

Unless the horse is a three-year-old colt or gelding, it must not have been in driving finishes in its last two races.

If the horse is four or older, its best effort at today's distance must not have occurred in its last race unless the horse is a male and the race was a Big Win.

The horse must not have lost more than two-and-a-half lengths in the stretch during its last race unless it had an alibi or was eased after showing high early speed.

Jockey

A horse is acceptable if its jockey (a) has won with it in the past, or (b) rates among the nation's leaders in terms of percentage of starts won during the previous year, or (c) rates among the nation's leaders with respect to money won during the previous year, or (d) either ranks among the top winners at the current meeting or has a winning average there of at least 16 percent.

If the jockey is an apprentice and has not won with the horse in the past, the horse remains acceptable if the rider is the hot apprentice of the current meeting or is listed among its leading riders provided (a) the horse is a front-runner and the race is to be run around only one turn, or (b) the boy has shown that he can win races around two turns on come-from-behind horses.

145

Weight

Find the horse's key race (see page 95).

If the horse is carrying no more weight than in the key race or if it is assigned 115 pounds or less, it is acceptable.

If the horse will carry up to 4 pounds more than in its key race and if today's impost is over 115 pounds, it can be accepted if it has ever won at today's distance or longer against company of today's class or better while carrying today's weight. If it has finished within two lengths of a winner while carrying higher weight, it can also be accepted.

If the horse will carry 5 pounds or more than in its key race, it is acceptable only if it meets the requirements of the above paragraph and also has raced within seven days or has had a workout within four.

If the horse is assigned 120 or more pounds today and did not carry within 2 pounds of today's weight in its key race, all the foregoing requirements must be met.

Class

No horse aged four or more is acceptable in handicaps or stakes unless it usually runs in them and has finished in the money when so entered.

A three-year-old can move from a Big Win in allowance company to a handicap—but not a stakes race—for horses of his own age, not older.

A two-year-old allowance winner is acceptable in a stakes.

A two-year-old winner of a maiden special is acceptable in an allowance but not in a stakes if other entrants have won stakes or allowance races at today's distance.

No horse aged three or more is acceptable in an allowance race unless it has done well against such company or is running today against horses similar to itself. One exception would be a lightly raced three-year-old which earned a good pace rating while winning a maiden special.

146

No horse can step up as much as 50 percent in claiming price (comparing its entered price last time with the highest price in today's race) unless it has won or finished within half a length of the winner in a race of today's class or higher at a track equal to today's.

A horse that has won nothing but a maiden claimer is not acceptable in a race for winners of two races or more unless it is a three-year-old that has run in the money in a regular claimer at a price not over $500 lower than today's.

Females

A filly or mare is acceptable in a race against males only if (a) it has beaten males of today's value at today's distance or longer, or (b) its key race was against males of today's value or higher, or (c) the key race was an f-claimer but the top claiming price of today's race is at least 20 percent lower than the price for which the female was entered in the key race.

No female is acceptable against males if the top claiming price today is $500 or more above the price for which the horse was entered in her last outing. If the last race was an f-claimer, reduce the listed price by 20 percent before making the comparison.

No female may step up any amount, against males or females, if it was in a driving finish in its last race and failed to gain ground in the stretch.

No female may step up from a claimer to an allowance or from an allowance to a handicap unless today's race is for females only and no other entrant has been able to win a race of today's class.

Consistency

Accept any horse with at least one win in seven to thirteen starts or two wins in fourteen or more starts this year. If it has had fewer than seven races this year, total its starts this year and last before making the computation.

The above requirement is waived for two-year-olds and for any horse that finished in the money or within a length of the winner

147

in its last race or had an alibi. The rule also is waived for a horse dropping at least $1,000 in claiming price to a level at which it has been able to win or finish within a length of the winner. It also is waived in maiden races.

Pace

With reference to the key race of each remaining contender, use a chart, a slide rule, or your own method to evaluate the leader's fractional time, the winner's final time, and the horse's final time. Add the three figures. This is the rating of the horse's key race (review pages 114–17).

Discard any horse entered in a sprint race if its rating is 10 points below those of at least two other contenders. If eliminating it would leave only one contender, hold off. A scratch might remove the top horse, and you would want a more complete study of the second horse.

Class Ratings

Give each contender the highest class rating it has earned at any major track in the past three months. Adjust the published values of the races according to the formula on pages 121–123.

Additional Eliminations

If you can eliminate more horses without leaving yourself with only one contender prior to the announcement of scratches, do so, this way:

Discard any horse whose pace and class ratings are each 10 points lower than those of another contender.

Discard all females whose pace and class ratings are not *superior* to those of all male contenders.

Before August 1, discard all three-year-olds running against older horses unless their pace and class ratings are superior. After August 1, accept a three-year-old if its combined pace and class ratings are greater than the combined ratings of each other contender.

Discard all horses aged eight or more unless their pace and class ratings are superior to those of all other contenders.

Discard any horse that lacks good early speed and is starting from an outside post position in a race around two turns.

Automatic Bets

If they are not scratched, and if they look ready when I see them in the paddock, I bet on the following kinds of horses without doing any additional paperwork:

A horse that (a) rates among the top three on pace and on pace plus class, and (b) is either the only front-runner among the remaining contenders, or (c) has a pace-setting style and usually gets to the half-mile call (in sprints) or the three-quarters (in routes) a fifth of a second or two more rapidly than any of the other contenders.

A horse that rates among the top three contenders, if it customarily runs slightly behind the early pace and is racing today against two or more highly pace-rated front-running types.

These two kinds of horses need not be checked for Plus Factors. If they run today, they are worth betting on. All other contenders should be checked for Plus Factors.

THE PLUS FACTORS

Except for the pace-rating and class-rating procedures, most of the foregoing material has been negative in purpose. Its object has been to find flaws justifying the elimination of horses from further study. Two or more horses may have survived these rigorous tests. If their pace and class ratings are fairly close and none of them qualifies as an automatic bet, some means must be found to determine whether one of them is a good bet by comparison with the others. At this point, the Plus Factors are an enormous help. Each Plus Factor refers to a positive achievement or powerful characteristic of the horse or a telltale maneuver by its trainer. Look for

149

these Plus Factors in the past-performance record of each contender. Whenever you find one, put a check next to the horse's name. If no automatic bet is available but one of the contenders earns four more Plus Factors than any of the others, it is likely to be a worthwhile bet. If two horses rate closely on pace and class and Plus Factors and the odds are right, you can bet both contenders. Here are the Plus Factors:

1. *Winning Favorite:* If the horse is listed as the favorite in the morning line of your racing paper or track program or if it becomes the favorite on the tote board, give it a check if it comes from a barn that customarily wins more than an average percentage of the races in which its horses go off as favorites (see pages 43–44).

2. *Consistent Stable:* Whether the horse is the favorite or not, give it a check if *The American Racing Manual* or the current list of leading trainers shows that its trainer qualifies as unusually consistent (see pages 40 and 41).

3. *Consistent Jockey:* If the rider is an unusually consistent winner, the horse deserves a check (see page 87). If the horse happens to be the favorite and you know that the jockey wins more than an average percentage of the races in which he rides favorites (page 87), the horse gets another check.

4. *Favorable Jockey Shift:* Check any contender that lost its last race but is to be ridden today by a different jockey, provided the boy is either one of the nation's leaders, or one of the leaders in the track's current standings, or has a winning percentage of 16 or better at this meeting or has won with the horse in the past. Also, if the horse is to be ridden today by the "hot" apprentice of the meeting, a check mark is given. A switch to a winning rider almost always means improvement, especially in a horse good enough to have come this far in the handicapping.

5. *Won Last Race Easily:* It probably retained enough energy for another good effort.

6. *Won Last Race Handily:* Ditto.

7. *Last Race Was a Big Win:* This kind of victory, described on

page 73, often gives assurance that another powerful performance is in store.

8. *Lost Last Race but Gained in Stretch:* The result chart or past-performance record may say something like "rallied" or "finished fast" or "gaining." Or in the absence of such comment, the record will show that the horse picked up at least two lengths in the stretch. For most horses a good finish indicates improving form.

9. *Lost Ground in the Middle Stages but Gained in Stretch:* The horse might have been blocked in the backstretch, losing ground in the middle stages of the race but retaining enough moxie to come again. The last race might look like this:

$$5 \quad 2 \quad 2^1 \quad 4^4 \quad 4^3 \quad 2^2$$

Even if the horse didn't fall back to fifth or sixth during the middle stages, it might lose a few lengths and regain most of them —or all of them—at the end. Such a horse often has better luck next time.

10. *Gained Three-and-a-Half Lengths or More in the Stretch:* A finishing kick of that magnitude gets an additional check.

11. *Displayed Early Speed:* If the horse led or was close to the early pace of its last race and was still in contention at the half-mile call or, in route races, at the three-quarters call, the evidence is comparable to that of a fast finish. It means that winning form is imminent. Naturally, some horses get out in front in all their races and quit every time. Such horses are not likely to last this long in my kind of handicapping.

12. *Has Won at Today's Distance by Leading at Every Call:* This suggests that when the horse is in winning shape, it gets out there and stays. If today is the day and the horse does it, he will avoid the traffic jams that often defeat slower-starting animals.

13. *Last Race Easy, Previous Race Good:* The last race was easy if the horse never challenged for the lead, finished fourth or worse, and earned comments such as "no excuse," "no mishap," "ran wide

all the way," "evenly," or "no rally." If everything else in the beast's record suggests that it can do well against today's cavalry and if its next-to-last race was a good one, you can safely assume that the last race was a deliberate breather.

14. *Alibi:* Because the betting public pays little attention to the reasons a horse loses—especially the reasons that qualify as alibis (see page 76), a horse that lost because of some misadventure may go off at nice odds today. Remember, a defeat may be attributable to poor racing luck or a bad ride by the jockey. It may also be the result if the trainer deliberately entered the horse in the wrong company or at the wrong distance, or with too much weight or in the mud.

15. *Last Race Within Seven Days of Today:* When a horse's record is good enough to qualify it for the Plus Factor study, you can be sure that a return to the starting gate seven days after its last outing is a sign that the stable is trying.

16. *Last Race Within Five Days of Today:* In big-time racing, five days is even better than seven and is worth an extra check.

17. *Today Is Second Start After Long Layoff or Long Trip:* Horses usually do much better in their second outing at a new track than in their first.

18. *Ran in Money After Long Layoff or Long Trip:* Same as above except that the horse was good enough to finish second or third in its return to the track. If the race did not involve an all-out drive and *especially* if the horse seemed "short"—which means that it didn't have much left in the stretch—it will probably improve today. If it won in a hard drive, I give it no check, fearing that the all-out effort after a long layoff or long journey may have set it back.

19. *Worked Out Yesterday:* Some of the best trainers give the horse a breezing workout the day before trying to win a purse.

20. *Recent Long Workout:* If the horse has been running short, tiring in the stretch, a six-furlong workout for today's sprint or a mile workout for today's route is a sign that the trainer has been

trying to put some bottom under the animal. The workout should have occurred three or more days ago to give the horse a chance to recover from it.

21. *Four Workouts in Past Twenty Days:* A horse that works out every three to five days is getting careful attention from its barn and is in good physical condition besides. (A Fred Davis contribution.)

22. *Six Pounds Less Weight than in Key Race:* If the trainer has found a spot in which the horse can go to the post with this much less weight than in its best race, you can be sure the trainer plans to cash in on the opportunity.

23. *Five Pounds Less Weight than in Last Race:* Like many horseplayers, some trainers are highly alert to "weight off" and "weight on," even when the last race was a totally different kind of proposition from today's. The reasoning here is similar to that in the item above. The trainer usually *likes* to get five pounds off and prepares his stock to take advantage of light imposts.

24. *Distance Switch:* Today the horse is running at a suitable distance. If the trainer had it at an unsuitable distance last time, the horse might have looked bad. The shorter or longer race probably improved the animal's condition, though, and it will be in shape to run a good race today.

25. *Steps Down in Class:* If the top claiming price for which horses can be entered in today's race is lower than the price at which the horse was entered in its last start, today's conditions are going to be easier.

26. *Steps Down an "Even" or Better Comment:* A horse that gallops home fourth, fifth, or sixth without much exertion (the trouble line will say "evenly"), and then steps down in class is a horse to watch. If it steps down after a race in which the trouble line was "good try" or "sharp" or "rallied," it probably is a stickout today.

27. *Steps Down Today and Also Stepped Down Last Time:* A horse dropped down repeatedly is a horse whose barn wants a

153

purse even if it has to lose the horse *via* a claim. The anxiety for a purse may be extraordinary because the stable is in hock. Or the dropping down may be an act of desperation because the horse is going bad. You will be able to tell all you need to know about this when you see the horse in the paddock. Meanwhile, give it a check.

28. *Stepped Down Last Time, Runs in Same Class Today:* The trainer seems to think the horse has found its proper level. If the horse did not qualify as a contender and did not have the pace and class ratings necessary before the handicapper bothers about its Plus Factors, the trainer's opinion would be of no consequence. But as matters stand, the animal rates a check. Today's race may indeed be exactly the kind it needs for a win.

29. *Up a Notch Last Start, Down Two Notches Today:* I think this is one of my two or three favorite Plus Factors. If the horse is entered today in a race with a top claiming price of $5,000, you may notice that the top two lines of its past-performance record look, in part, like this:

Clm 6000
Clm 5500

First it was stepped up a notch, from $5,500 to $6,000, and now it is dropping two notches to $5,000. This kind of thing is often accompanied by jockey and distance switches, alibis, and other lucrative kinds of manipulation.

30. *Drops from Claimer to f-Claimer Without Face-Value Drop:* A mare entered today against $5,000 fillies and mares is dropping in class if its last race was against $5,000 colts and geldings. If you bother to test my 20 percent formula for evaluating the class of f-claimers (see page 103) and if you know how the crowd overlooks this kind of thing, you will appreciate this Plus Factor.

31. *Drops from Claimer to f-Claimer with Apparent Value Rise:* Applying the same formula, it can be seen that a mare that ran last time in a Clm 5000 is by no means stepping up in class if today's race is an f-6000. It gets a check mark.

154

32. *In New Low Class Today:* A horse that qualifies as a contender deserves a check if it is running against the easiest prey of its career.

33. *Has Never Been Beaten by More than Half a Length at This Distance When Running in Today's Class or Lower:* Another sign that the trainer may have found The Spot today.

34. *Highest Class Rating:* If one horse is superior to the other contenders in terms of class, it should get credit.

35. *Highest Class Rating by 15 Points:* A $1,500 bulge in the class department deserves an extra check.

36. *Has Won Allowance Race at Major Track:* This is a great sign in any claiming race and is often a good sign in cheaper allowance races.

37. *Has Won a Handicap Race at Major Track:* Ditto as far as claiming, allowance, and handicap races are concerned. Do not be afraid to give a horse check marks for this item AND the one above if it earns them.

38. *Recently Claimed:* There are circumstances in which recently claimed horses are poison. The previous terms of the present handicapping method are such, however, as to rule out that any horse will run over its head today—as so many recently claimed horses are forced to do by the rules of racing. If you adhere to the principles propounded in this book, you can unhesitatingly check any horse claimed within the last month provided it has not won since being claimed.

39. *Drops Below Price at Which It Was Claimed:* If the creature was claimed within the past three months and today is racing for the first time at a price lower than the one at which it was bought, you know that the new proprietors are stopping at nothing to cadge a purse. Naturally, the horse may have gone sour. If so, a paddock inspection will almost certainly reveal that fact, and the horse will be eliminated. Pending that inspection, it gets a check.

40. *Consistency:* If the horse has won 20 percent of its starts and has averaged at least $500 an outing in a total of at least six races

155

this year (or this year and last combined if it has run fewer than six times this year), you can be sure it is a good bet today. Consistency is among the most potent of Plus Factors when the consistent horse has good pace and class ratings.

41. *Only Consistent Horse:* The consistent horse rates an additional credit if it is the only such horse among the contenders.

42. *Gelding:* Colts beat geldings every day, and so do fillies and mares. But a gelding in shape to run its best is the most reliable of Thoroughbreds. Give it a check.

43. *Entry:* A contender coupled in the betting with another horse is a contender with something extra going for it. The stable will almost certainly use the other horse to help create the kind of pace situation most favorable to the contender. In fact, if the contender is a come-from-behind type and the stablemate is a front-runner and the entry's main rival is another front-runner, I give two checks.

44. *Fast Final Quarter:* The late Colonel E. R. Bradley used to make a lot of money betting on horses that had run the last quarter-mile of a recent race in 24 seconds or less. He believed that a horse able to finish that quickly in a six-furlong race was a good risk at any distance in its next start. A horse that finished in 24 seconds in a mile race was a good bet at any distance from the mile on up, the Colonel thought. I have checked this wrinkle for years and have found that it works extraordinarily well if the horse in question qualifies on other, more fundamental principles of handicapping. Anybody who cannot tell whether a horse has run the last quarter-mile of a six-furlong race in 24 seconds or better is advised to drop everything and learn how to read past-performance records. For those who know but do not know that they know, here is a sample:

$$45 \quad 1.09\tfrac{4}{5} \quad 1 \quad 5 \quad 5^4 \quad 5^5 \quad 3^3 \quad 2^1$$

The quarter-mile between the half-mile fraction and the finish line of this particular race was clocked in $24\tfrac{4}{5}$ seconds. But the horse itself gained four lengths during those two furlongs, covering the ground in 24 seconds flat. If it is entered today at the right distance (which it is), it gets *not one but two checks*. This is a mighty powerful wrinkle, and two checks is by no means overgenerous. The only condition, other than the 24-second final quarter, is that the feat must have occurred within the last month and the horse must not have won a race since.

Unless you do your handicapping from official results charts, you will be able to work this angle only on races of six furlongs and a mile. The *Daily Racing Form* past performances give reasonably exact running positions and clockings at the half-mile call of six-furlong races and the three-quarter call in mile races. But at other distances it is impossible to tell how fast the final quarter was run.

45. *Maiden Ran Second:* In a maiden race for three-year-olds and up, a horse that finished second in its latest start deserves a check. Fred Davis shows in his classic *Percentages and Probabilities* that such animals make up less than 10 percent of these fields yet win one out of four of the races—almost three times the statistical expectation. A powerful factor.

46. *Top Speed in Sprint:* Give a check to a sprint contender who rates among the top three when the better of each starter's latest two speed ratings are compared. Davis shows that almost two-thirds of sprints are won by such a horse.

47. *Stakes Class:* In an allowance race, check any contender who has so much as started in a stakes race and has never been in a claiming race. Fred Davis shows that although these are barely a quarter of the starters in such races, they account for almost half the victories.

48. *Allowance Consistency:* In an allowance race, check a contender who has won at least two of its latest six starts.

49. *Mud Mark:* When the track is sloppy, muddy, or heavy, check a contender whose past-performance record includes a *Daily Racing Form* mud mark.

So much for the Plus Factors. So much, indeed, for the paper work of handicapping. If you have been careful, and if it is a good day of racing, you may have found three or four races that strike you as playable. You will have jotted down the names of the contenders and the pace and class ratings and the number of check marks each one earned. You will go to the paddock, see the horses, and make your decision.

Will you win? Probably not right away, except by accident. Like everything else worthwhile except the inheritance of a fortune from a rich relative, handicapping skill has to be earned. It takes effort and experience. But when it is earned, when you can at last distinguish a playable race from an unplayable one, when you can narrow the field to its real contention and can pick the actual winner at least four of every ten times, you will have a lucrative hobby.

I guarantee you no more than that. But has anybody else guaranteed you even that much lately?

Harriet Beecher Stowe's
UNCLE TOM'S CABIN

Edited and with an Introduction by
HAROLD BLOOM

First Printing
1 3 5 7 9 8 6 4 2

ISBN: 0-7910-3697-9

Chelsea House Publishers
1974 Sproul Road, Suite 400
P.O. Box 914
Broomall, PA 19008-0914

Contents

User's Guide

This volume is designed to present biographical, critical, and bibliographical information on Harriet Beecher Stowe and *Uncle Tom's Cabin*. Following Harold Bloom's introduction, there appears a detailed biography of the author, discussing the major events in her life and her important literary works. Then follows a thematic and structural analysis of the work, in which significant themes, patterns, and motifs are traced. An annotated list of characters supplies brief information on the chief characters in the work.

A selection of critical extracts, derived from previously published material by leading critics, then follows. The extracts consist of statements by the author on her work, early reviews of the work, and later evaluations down to the present day. The items are arranged chronologically by date of first publication. A bibliography of Stowe's writings (including a complete listing of all books she wrote, cowrote, edited, and translated), a list of additional books and articles on her and on *Uncle Tom's Cabin,* and an index of themes and ideas conclude the volume.

Harold Bloom is Sterling Professor of the Humanities at Yale University and Henry W. and Albert A. Berg Professor of English at the New York University Graduate School. He is the author of twenty books and the editor of more than thirty anthologies of literature and literary criticism.

Professor Bloom's works include *Shelley's Mythmaking* (1959), *The Visionary Company* (1961), *Blake's Apocalypse* (1963), *Yeats* (1970), *A Map of Misreading* (1975), *Kabbalah and Criticism* (1975), and *Agon: Towards a Theory of Revisionism* (1982). *The Anxiety of Influence* (1973) sets forth Professor Bloom's provocative theory of the literary relationships between the great writers and their predecessors. His most recent books are *The American Religion* (1992) and *The Western Canon* (1994).

Professor Bloom earned his Ph.D. from Yale University in 1955 and has served on the Yale faculty since then. He is a 1985 MacArthur Foundation Award recipient and served as the Charles Eliot Norton Professor of Poetry at Harvard University in 1987–88. He is currently the editor of the Chelsea House series Major Literary Characters and Modern Critical Views, and other Chelsea House series in literary criticism.

Introduction

HAROLD BLOOM

Uncle Tom's Cabin or, Life among the Lowly was published on March 20, 1852, and by about a year after its publication was reported to have sold over 300,000 copies in the United States and well over another two million throughout the world, both in the original and in translation. As Edmund Wilson noted, it lost almost all its popularity after the Civil War (which it had helped to cause), and did not regain a wide audience until the second half of our century. Wilson speculated that both sides, North and South, did not want to be reminded of the Issue of black slavery for nearly a century after Emancipation. And yet, rereading it now, I have to agree with Wilson that it is a permanent and impressive work, forceful and fierce, a book worthy of the spirit of John Brown, who prophetically warned the nation: "Without the shedding of blood, there is no remission of sins." As a narrative, *Uncle Tom's Cabin* has its weaknesses, but the book is powerful in its characterizations. Wilson shrewdly said that the characters "express themselves a good deal better than the author expresses herself." I find this to be particularly true of Aunt Chloe and Uncle Tom, of Eliza and of George Harris and, most of all, of that magnificent and mythological monster, the superbly wicked Simon Legree, a plantation owner yet a New England Yankee, as Wilson reminded us.

Harriet Beecher Stowe, though moved by a biblical sense of urgency, was too shrewd to write her book as a mere polemic against the South. Her concerns, and her anguish, were patriotic but national, and *Uncle Tom's Cabin* indicts both North and South, in the name of Christianity. Because an "Uncle Tom" has become a black and liberal term of contempt, we need to begin reading the book by cleansing ourselves of our period prejudices. Uncle Tom is not only the novel's heroic protagonist but indeed is the only authentic Christian in Stowe's vision of her nation. A literary character greatly admired by Tolstoy and by Dickens deserves our careful regard. For Stowe, Uncle Tom is the Christ-like martyr more truly crucified by the North than by the South, for New England had accepted the Fugitive Slave Act of 1850, and Simon Legree is, for Stowe, the diabolic incarnation of that hideous surrender of Yankee integrity. The last paragraph of the novel, still intense, peals out a prophecy worthy of John Brown himself:

> A day of grace is yet held out to us. Both North and South have been guilty before God; and the *Christian church* has a heavy account to answer. Not by combining together, to protect injustice and cruelty, and making a common capital of sin, is this Union to be saved,—but by repentance, justice and mercy; for, not surer is the eternal law by which the millstone sinks in the ocean, than that stronger law, by which injustice and cruelty shall bring on nations the wrath of Almighty God!

Some critics have remarked that Uncle Tom's Christian forbearance is unpersuasive to them, since it seems more than human. Perhaps the character *is* a touch more than human; there is a biblical grandeur to him that his utterances almost consistently earn. But he is more myth (in the positive sense) than cartoon or caricature, and the book's context sustains his martyrdom. Simon Legree doubtless is more persuasive: He owes something to the Puritan spirit in its decadence and decline, and he has his affinities to that other great devil, Hawthorne's Chillingworth in *The Scarlet Letter*. It is exactly accurate, aesthetically and spiritually, that his greatest hatred for Tom is caused by the slave's overwhelmingly sincere Christianity. The savage gusto of Stowe's villain was caught up splendidly in Vachel Lindsay's "Simon Legree—A Negro Sermon," the first of three poems that he dedicated to the memory of Booker T. Washington. Lindsay's chant concludes with a mad glee that Stowe might not have appreciated, and yet it testifies to the lasting imaginative power that had created Simon Legree:

> And the Devil said to Simon Legree:
> "I like your style, so wicked and free.
> Come sit and share my throne with me,
> And let us bark and revel."
> And there they sit and gnash their teeth,
> And each one wears a hop-vine wreath.
> They are matching pennies and shooting craps,
> They are playing poker and taking naps.
> And old Legree is fat and fine:
> He eats the fire, he drinks the wine—
> Blood and burning turpentine—
> *Down, down with the Devil;*
> *Down, down with the Devil;*
> *Down, down with the Devil.* ✤

Biography of Harriet Beecher Stowe

Harriet Elizabeth Beecher was born in Litchfield, Connecticut, on June 14, 1811, the daughter of the Reverend Lyman and Roxana Beecher and sister of Henry Ward Beecher, the celebrated clergyman, author, and editor. She underwent a severe religious upbringing by her stern and tyrannical father, who was a follower of Jonathan Edwards, preaching hellfire and damnation in his thunderous lectures and scorning the female members of his family. Harriet herself, although remaining deeply religious throughout her life, developed a much milder and more benificent Christian temperament. After her mother's death in 1816 she came under the influence of her eldest sister Catherine, who a few years later set up a school in Hartford where Harriet was first a student and later a teacher.

Harriet began writing in the mid-1820s; among her earliest works are a theological essay and an unfinished blank-verse tragedy, *Cleon* (1825). In 1832 the family moved to Cincinnati, Ohio, where Lyman Beecher became president of the Lane Theological Seminary and Catherine Beecher founded a college for women, the Western Female Institute. Harriet was an assistant at the institute until the school closed in 1837. On January 6, 1836, Harriet married Calvin Ellis Stowe, a professor of biblical literature at her father's seminary. They would eventually have seven children; one of them died in the cholera epidemic of 1849 and another was drowned in 1857. Harriet's first publications were stories written for the *Western Monthly Magazine* in 1833; initially her motives for writing were no loftier than to provide money for her family. In 1843 she published *The Mayflower; or, Sketches of Scenes and Characters among the Descendants of the Pilgrims.*

Harriet Beecher Stowe gained her first direct knowledge of slavery while living in Cincinnati. Kentucky, a slave state, lay just across the Ohio River, and Ohioans were divided in their response to runaway slaves, some believing they should be returned to their owners. Both the Beechers and the Stowes were opposed to slavery and eventually joined the abolitionist cause. Harriet and Calvin Stowe once took into their home a little girl who claimed she was free. When her master came to claim her the Stowes helped her escape at night.

In 1850 Stowe moved to Brunswick, Maine, where her husband had been appointed professor at Bowdoin College. There she wrote her antislavery novel *Uncle Tom's Cabin*, serialized in the *National Era* in 1851–52 and published in book form in 1852. The novel was a tremendous success and was translated into at least twenty-three languages. It was, however, violently attacked in the slave-holding South (and also by some newspapers in the North), so in 1853 Stowe published *A Key to* Uncle Tom's Cabin to demonstrate the factual basis for her book. She followed *Uncle Tom's Cabin* with a second antislavery novel, *Dred: A Tale of the Great Dismal Swamp* (1856), based in part on the Nat Turner slave uprising in 1831; but it was very poorly received. As a means of escaping from the vilification she was suffering in the press, Stowe visited Europe in 1853, 1856, and 1859. Her travel impressions were written up in *Sunny Memories of Foreign Lands* (1854).

Uncle Tom's Cabin and the Civil War made Harriet Beecher Stowe a celebrity and her name a household word. When she called on Abraham Lincoln at the White House, he greeted her by saying, "So this is the little lady who made this big war." John William DeForest, writing in the *Nation* in 1868, first used the phrase "The Great American Novel" to describe *Uncle Tom's Cabin.* Stowe, however, did not participate much in the Civil War, although her son Frederick William volunteered on the Union side and was seriously injured at Gettysburg. After the war she wrote a number of sketches of "leading patriots of the day" (all on the Union cause, and including Abraham Lincoln, Frederick Douglass, and her brother Henry Ward Beecher), published as *Men of Our Times* (1868). She also turned her attention to journalism, contributing frequently to the newly founded *Atlantic Monthly.* The association was profitable for both until the publication in 1869 of Stowe's "The True Story of Lady Byron's Life," a sympathetic representation of Lady Byron's separation from the poet and their marital difficulties, including Byron's incestuous relationship with his half-sister. The story lost the magazine 15,000 subscribers and dealt a heavy blow to Stowe's national prestige. Undeterred, she expanded the article to book length and published it as *Lady Byron Vindicated* in 1870.

In 1852 the Stowes had moved to Andover, Massachusetts. After Calvin Stowe's retirement in 1864 from the theological seminary there, the family moved to Hartford, Connecticut. Stowe's novels of this period are chronicles of New England life: *The Minister's Wooing* (1859), *The Pearl of Orr's Island* (1862), *Oldtown Folks* (1869), and *Poganuc People* (1878). From 1868 to 1884 the Stowes spent the winter in Florida, where Harriet assisted in the cause of Reconstruction. Her descriptive sketches of Florida were collected as *Palmetto-Leaves* (1873). She also wrote a number of stories for children (*Queer Little People*, 1867; *Little Pussy Willow*, 1870) and domestic novels (*My Wife and I*, 1871; *Pink and White Tyranny*, 1871; *We and Our Neighbors*, 1875), which elaborate upon some points raised in a treatise she wrote with her sister Catherine, *The American Woman's Home* (1869).

Stowe's neighbor for the last twenty years of her life was Mark Twain, who reported poignantly on her increasing physical and mental deterioration in her later years. Harriet Beecher Stowe died in Hartford on July 1, 1896. ❖

Thematic and Structural Analysis

In the short **preface** to *Uncle Tom's Cabin,* Harriet Beecher Stowe adopts a tendentious authorial voice that marks her novel as a call to reform. In abolitionist diction, highly moral and just as sentimental, Stowe advises the reader that "the object of these sketches is to awaken sympathy and feeling for the African race, as they exist among us," in pre–Civil War America. Slavery is the overarching evil to be eradicated, yet stereotypes of African Americans permeate the text from its first sentence, and the cultural superiority of the "dominant Anglo-Saxon race" is never in question. Through the experiences of various protagonists, the themes of the novel pivot upon a Christian model of suffering and redemption, the acts of the moral individual and the corresponding failure of a democratic society, and the troubling replacement of racist cruelty by racist benevolence. *Uncle Tom's Cabin* is a narrative of its time, but it offers to the modern critical reader insight into the pervasive effects of slavery upon American culture.

In **chapter one** we overhear two Kentucky men negotiating the sale of several slaves, including Uncle Tom and a four-year-old quadroon boy, Harry. Haley, the slave trader, and Mr. Shelby, their owner, are contrasts in appearance and caste. The former is a coarse, obviously prosperous man involved in a perfectly legal, if distasteful, business; the latter is a gentleman who calls himself "humane" and "hate[s] to take the boy from his mother," but must, after all, pay his debts. Haley reminds Mr. Shelby that a critical difference between slaves and "white folks" is that slaves cannot—and do not—expect to keep their wives and children. Stowe tells us that Kentucky has "the mildest form" of slavery and that the apparent ease and stability of slave life may deceive a visitor into believing that slavery is a benign "patriarchal institution."

Harry's mother, Eliza, overhears the slave trader's offer for her son and, astonished and distraught, appeals to her mistress. Mrs. Shelby knows nothing of her husband's financial difficulties, nor can she imagine that he would sell his slaves. She assures Eliza that the sale of Harry is as unthinkable as that of her own children.

In **chapters two and three** Stowe depicts the dependence of the slave family upon those who own them. Eliza, the "petted and indulged favorite" of her mistress, is a gracious, refined, and beautiful mulatto married to George Harris, a mulatto slave on a nearby plantation. And although the couple had been married in the Shelbys' parlor, with "white gloves, and cake and wine," Eliza and George are at the mercy of the whims and indulgences of their owners. George is hired out by his master to work in a factory and invents an agricultural device, which earns him the admiration of his employer and the resentment of his master, who abruptly returns him to the "meanest drudgery" on the farm. Furious over his mistreatment, George reveals to his wife his plans to run away to Canada, where he will work, save money, and buy his family from Mr. Shelby. Unaware that their child has been sold, Eliza, who equates obedience to her master and mistress with Christian commitment, urges him to have faith and forbearance. George has less gentle thoughts, demanding, as if of God, "Who made this man my master?"

Stowe abruptly shifts scenes—as she does frequently in the novel—to Tom and his wife, Chloe, presiding over a humble and "respectable" domesticity within their own cabin on the Shelby plantation (**chapter four**). Tom's African features are "characterized by an expression of grave and steady good sense, united with much kindliness and benevolence." As Chloe cooks dinner he struggles to write, instructed by "Mas'r George," the Shelbys' thirteen-year-old son, and a love of home and of children pervades the slave cabin. Tom is a sort of local religious patriarch: After dinner, slaves arrive from surrounding plantations for worship and singing. At the same time, Mr. Shelby and the slave trader conclude their business in the master's house. Haley assures Shelby he will sell Tom into good hands.

Shelby's debts are cleared, and he informs his wife of the transaction (**chapter five**). She reacts strongly, urging her husband to make "a pecuniary sacrifice" to settle his debt rather than sell Tom and Harry, but he insists that "there is no choice between selling these two and selling everything." Mrs. Shelby resolves to see the slaves in person rather than arrange to be away when they are taken, as her husband suggests.

Eliza overhears the Shelbys' conversation and prepares to run away with her child. She stops at Tom's cabin to tell him that he has been sold and will be taken in the morning. Tom realizes that his value as a slave will be sufficient to save others from being sold and that by running he would doom them all. Eliza asks Tom and Chloe to tell her husband that she will try to reach Canada and meet him there.

Chapter six opens the next morning when the Shelbys discover that Eliza has run off with her child. Mr. Shelby, his honor at stake, rushes off to calm Haley and to offer his horses and servants for a search. With the complicity of Mrs. Shelby, the other slaves—in a rather comical interlude—conspire to hinder the search.

In **chapters seven and eight** maternal love is a powerful force strong enough to overcome desolation, cold, and fierce pursuit. In a scene that would become a literary symbol of female peril and endangerment, Eliza escapes across the Ohio River, literally one step ahead of the slave trader. Shoeless and bleeding, she clutches her child and jumps across huge chunks of broken ice. Throughout the novel slaves endure hardship and danger as a matter of course, but they must redeem themselves out of slavery by extraordinary acts of courage and spiritual strength.

A stranger helps Eliza up the Ohio bank and directs her to a nearby house where fugitive slaves are protected. A "poor, heathenish man," the stranger is impressed by her courage and exclaims that she has earned her liberty. Stowe dryly remarks that had the man been "better situated and more enlightened," he would have known not to assist an escaping slave.

Meanwhile Haley, having been forced to abandon his pursuit of Eliza, takes refuge in a nearby tavern. There he meets his former partner, Tom Loker, and Loker's new partner, Marks. He arranges for the men to catch the escaped mother and child. In payment, they will be "given" Eliza to sell in New Orleans.

In **chapter nine** the divergence of legislative and moral imperatives is evidenced in the passing of the Fugitive Slave Act of 1850, under which the North was no longer a legal haven for runaways and Canada became the closest place of freedom. The reader is introduced to Senator Bird of Ohio, who defends the act to his unsympathetic wife, Mary, claiming that it will keep peace with Kentucky slave owners. Mary vows to break this law at the first opportunity. Although the senator admires her conviction, he makes a distinction between feelings and judgment when political unrest may be alleviated by legal compromise. But the appearance of Eliza and her child, needy and pathetic, appeals more strongly to his moral sense than an abstract, legalistic image of a runaway slave: "[H]is idea of a fugitive was only an idea of the letters that spell the word. . . . The magic of the real presence of distress . . . these [images] he had never tried." Eliza's journey continues as the senator secretly takes her to the home of a man who has freed all his own slaves and now protects others. Senator Bird gives the man money for Eliza and Harry's needs and leaves to resume his legislator's duties in Columbus.

We return to Tom's cabin on the Shelby plantation as he prepares for the arrival of the slave trader (**chapter ten**). Stowe invests Tom with a "gentle, domestic heart," "characteristic of his unhappy race." He knows that this is the last time he will see his children, since few return from the southernmost plantations. Africans, whose "instinctive affections" are "peculiarly strong," whisper in terror among themselves about being "sold south." Escape to Canada requires that the slave overcome a "naturally patient, timid and unenterprising" character. Tom is an anomaly that Stowe defines carefully. Neither fearful nor timid, he is an archetypal passive resister whose eyes are always turned toward God. Honorable in all things, Tom will not ruin his master's credit with the slave trader by running away.

Haley leaves, having shackled Tom to prevent his escape. Young "Mas'r George" catches up to the wagon and vows to come after Tom and bring him back to Kentucky.

Chapter eleven opens in a small country hotel where a traveler, Mr. Wilson, comes across a handbill advertising a reward for the capture or killing of a runaway slave (George Harris). The reader learns that Wilson is the manufacturer to whom George was hired out before his escape. Soon after, a stranger enters the inn and requests a room. Wilson recognizes the man, despite his disguise as a white gentleman of property, as George. Later, in George's quarters, Wilson urges him not to risk his life by breaking the laws of his country. "Sir," George replies, "I haven't any country. . . . But I'm going to have one . . . when I get to Canada, where the laws will own me and protect me, *that* shall be my country." Moved, Wilson offers George money and promises to deliver a token to Eliza when he returns home.

In **chapter twelve** the slave auction concludes, Haley takes Tom and his other human purchases onto a riverboat, and they begin a hellish journey south. Elegant white travelers comment upon the condition of the "Negro"; a clergyman manipulates Scripture to justify slavery; a mother tells her questioning child that although the separation of families is a "bad thing," it doesn't happen often enough to matter, and slaves are better off than they would be if free; a delicate and intelligent young minister predicts that God will bring Haley "into judgment"; a slave drowns herself after the sale of her infant son, and Haley records her death in his account book as a loss. The author interjects with the observation that "the enlightened, cultivated, intelligent" man is as much to blame for tolerating slavery as the trader for dealing in it.

In **chapter thirteen** we learn that Eliza and her child have found shelter in a Quaker settlement in Ohio and that the Quakers are making arrangements to secure their safe passage. While there, they are reunited with George, and they prepare to leave after sundown.

Tom's journey south continues, and he meets the spiritually precocious white child, Evangeline St. Clare (**chapter fourteen**). In the character of Little Eva, as she is called, Stowe concentrates a religious and moral clarity that the text suggests is possible only in children and in the darkest Africans. Eva and Tom become friends after he saves her from drowning, and her father, a Louisiana plantation owner, purchases Tom at her request. The story of Augustine St. Clare and his family, continuing through chapter twenty-nine, describes the effects of a brutal system upon both masters and slaves. St. Clare is an impractical and tenderhearted skeptic, liberal and indulgent with his slaves, his hypochondriac wife, and his daughter. His forty-five-year-old cousin, Ophelia, travels with them from her home in Vermont to look after the delicate Eva and to help manage the household during his wife's frequent illnesses.

Ophelia St. Clare is "a living impersonation of order, method, and exactness." Well read and energetic, she is a firm believer in duty, religion, the abolition of slavery, and the proper training of children. Augustine, Ophelia, Eva, and Tom arrive at the plantation (**chapter fifteen**). Eva rhapsodizes on the beauty of her home, but to Ophelia it seems "old and heathenish." Tom, by his link to a lush and splendid African exoticism, Stowe tells us, is comfortable here. Eva greets "Mammy," a "decent mulatto woman," with repeated kisses, and the affection is returned without restraint. Ophelia remarks to Augustine that she could not kiss a slave as Eva does. In **chapter sixteen** Marie St. Clare, the languid image of decayed, effete Southern attitudes, counters Ophelia's criticism of her having separated Mammy from her husband and children when she married and moved from her father's plantation. "Don't you believe that the Lord made them of one blood with us?" Ophelia asks. "No, indeed, not I!" Marie replies, later elaborating, "And just as if Mammy could love her little dirty babies as I love Eva!" Augustine counters with his distinction between simple love for one's fellow man and the abstract benevolence of the Northern abolitionists: "You loathe them as you would a snake or a toad, yet you are indignant at their wrongs. You would not have them abused; but you don't want to have anything to do with them yourselves."

In **chapter seventeen** preparations continue at the Ohio Quaker settlement to help George and Eliza escape to Canada with their child. Once on their way, they are pursued by traders Loker and Marks. Trapped with their Quaker guide in an isolated range of rocks, the former slaves defend themselves with George's pistols by firing on the party below. Loker is injured and deserted by his party; the fugitives continue their journey after leaving Loker in the care of nearby Quakers.

Like the suicide on the riverboat, another mother is destroyed by loss in **chapter eighteen**. Prue, who brings breads for sale to the St. Clare plantation, is a known drinker. She tells Tom that her life has been spent as a breeder of children who were all sold "as fast as they got big enough." She had hoped to keep the last one but, forbidden by her mistress to feed it, was unable to keep it alive. "I tuck to drinkin', to keep its crying out of my ears! I did,—and I will drink!" she tells Tom, as he tries to comfort her with promises of heaven. Since heaven is "where white folks is gwine," Prue prefers hell. In **chapter nineteen** she dies, locked in a cellar by her master. Ophelia confronts St. Clare about legal protections for the likes of Prue. He replies that there is no law to protect a slave and that the only "resource" is to ignore the excesses of barbarous people.

Chapter twenty introduces Topsy, a neglected, unloved, troublesome young slave girl. Dispensing with any natural attachment to parents or to God, she tells Ophelia, "I spect I grow'd. Don't think nobody never made me." Despite her constant professions of uncontrollable "wickedness," her inept thievery, and some pathological lying, we discover that Topsy is as pure of heart as Little Eva. Dark-skinned, with a "goblin-like" face and twinkling eyes, she retains a sense of self and a peculiar dignity, although her short life has been bereft of love. St. Clare has purchased the girl for Ophelia to mold as she wishes, challenging his cousin to fulfill her Northern abolitionist ideals. Eva and Topsy become friends and playmates.

The scene then shifts to the Shelby plantation, where Tom's wife, Aunt Chloe, is hired out as a baker in Louisville (**chapter twenty-one**). The Shelbys agree to hold her wages toward buying back her husband.

In **chapter twenty-two** we see Tom and Eva again after two years have passed. By this time they have become nearly inseparable and Eva's health has deteriorated from "that soft, insidious disease" that we later learn is tuberculosis. She expresses her wish to free all of her family's slaves and to teach them to read and write, but this idea meets with ridicule from her mother. **Chapter twenty-three** introduces St. Clare's twin brother, Alfred, and his son, Henrique, who have arrived on a visit. Their unrelenting cruelty toward their slaves stands in sharp contrast to Eva's simple love of fellow man and St. Clare's ideal of true democracy.

Eva weakens rapidly and tells Tom and St. Clare that she is dying (**chapter twenty-four**). She implores her father to "go all round and try to persuade people to do right" about slavery, to "have all slaves made free." Eva tells her friend Topsy that Ophelia would love her if only she were good, to which Topsy simply replies, "No; she can't bar me, 'cause I'm a nigger" (**chapter twenty-five**). The ruthless clarity of the child's understanding cuts through the rhetoric of religious ideality and moral sentiment. St. Clare overhears the children and makes a Christian metaphor literal in order to translate Eva's message of love for Ophelia. He reminds his cousin that Christ had put his hands on the blind in order to give them sight. Ophelia admits that she is repulsed by Topsy's touch, yet she imagines, incorrectly, that the child is insensitive to it. "[H]ow can I help feeling so?" she asks. St. Clare speculates that Ophelia, an "old disciple," might learn from Eva, the younger one.

Eva's dying is a long and melodramatic process that evokes the pathos common in deaths by tuberculosis in nineteenth-century novels (**chapter twenty-six**). Her bedroom is filled with objects intended to bring only "heart soothing and beautiful thoughts," and she reads her Bible as much as her failing strength will allow. Topsy brings flowers, and the insufferable Marie cannot understand the affection between the children. Eva again tries, without success, to convince her mother that Topsy is not inherently wicked but has been unloved until now, and that the child wants to be good. Tom spends much time with Eva in her illness. They are kindred spirits, alike in religious faith and in imagination.

The effects of Eva's death are immediate upon the household members (**chapter twenty-seven**). As Topsy mourns the death of the only person who has ever loved her, Ophelia is moved, at last, to love her young student. St. Clare wonders what he may do in response to the lesson of Little Eva's goodness. In his emptiness he turns to Tom and admits that he wants to believe the Bible but cannot. Tom says that he would give his life if it would make "Mas'r" a Christian.

Although religious faith eludes him, St. Clare becomes more practical and circumspect in the management of his slaves and informs Tom that he will emancipate him (**chapter twenty-eight**). Ophelia asks Augustine to make Topsy legally hers, and her cousin reminds her that she will then be a slaveholder and a "backsliding" abolitionist. But Ophelia understands that Topsy must have an owner to protect her and that by owning her she will then be able to bring her to the "free states" and give her liberty. But Topsy's emancipation papers are the only such papers St. Clare completes: He dies soon after, stabbed by a stranger. His master's habitual negligence dooms Tom, as Marie ignores her husband's desire to emancipate him and decides to sell all the slaves but Topsy (**chapter twenty-nine**). Ophelia writes to the Shelbys on Tom's behalf in an effort to save him from auction.

The scene in the slave warehouse, described in **chapter thirty**, is Stowe's most powerful and deftly drawn portrayal of the pervasiveness of the slave trade in America. Human property is valuable, so this New Orleans facility is a neatly kept house where slaves are fed and groomed for market "separately or in lots, to suit the convenience of the purchaser." Stowe carefully describes how the head of a "respectable" Northern firm, having become the creditor of a Southern plantation owner, is compelled to become involved in slave trade to recoup his losses: "He didn't like trading in slaves and souls of men . . . but, then, there were thirty thousand dollars in the case, and that was rather too much money to be lost for a principle."

A refined and "respectably dressed" mulatto woman and her fifteen-year-old quadroon daughter are among the lot to be sold with the St. Clare slaves. Susan and her daughter, Emmeline, have been brought up as Christians. The girl is expected to bring a high price for her beauty, and Stowe compares the mother's feelings to those of "any other Christian mother," except that she will find no refuge in religious or moral principle: The man who will receive the profits for the sale of the two women is a Northerner and a Christian. Susan is bought by a kindly man who tries to buy Emmeline as well, but he is outbid by Simon Legree, who also buys Tom.

The barbarousness with which female slaves in particular were "evaluated" and sold is also plainly evident in Stowe's slave auction scene. Although at the time any African ancestry legally designated one a "Negro," female slaves with traces of European ancestry were prized for their exotic beauty. The scene in which Legree, before the sale, runs his hands appraisingly over Emmeline's body would be outrageous and obscene to polite nineteenth-century readers—except that Emmeline is a slave of racially mixed blood.

Since the publication of *Uncle Tom's Cabin*, Simon Legree's name has, for good reason, become synonymous with evil and cunning. In **chapters thirty-one and thirty-two** Legree and the new slaves arrive at a place of cypress swamps, snakes, mournful wind, and rotting vegetation after a grueling boat trip upriver. Here slaves work without comfort and with only the meanest provisions and shelter. They rise at dawn to pick cotton; they eat at midnight. Still, Tom's faith in God remains unshakable, and in dreams Little Eva reads to him from the Bible. He works diligently in the fields and waits, with "religious patience," for some way of escape.

A strange woman joins the slaves at work in the fields in **chapter thirty-three**. Her delicate features and graceful bearing, good clothing, and scornful pride distinguish her among the ragged and hungry slaves as she picks cotton with fierce speed and skill. The woman, Cassy, initially does not speak but keeps close to Tom, as if sensing his singular strength. Tom helps a weakened woman unable to keep up with the fast pace of the work by filling her sack with his own cotton. Cassy muses that he will abandon all kindness once he realizes how hard it is to take care of himself in this place. "The Lord never visits these parts," she bitterly remarks.

Late in the evening the slaves return to a building where the cotton is weighed and collected by Simon Legree. He offers Tom a promotion to slave driver if he will flog the woman he had helped that day in the field. Tom refuses and Legree violently batters him, asking if the Bible does not order servants to obey their masters. "[M]y soul an't yours, Mas'r," Tom replies. Badly beaten, Tom lies alone in the refuse room of the gin-house, where Cassy comes to care for him (**chapter thirty-**

four). As she tends his wounds and soothes his pain she urges him to give up hope in God. She tells him that she has lived, "body and soul," with Legree for five years and that now he has "a new one," whom the reader already knows as Emmeline. She argues against Tom's hope with the story of her own despair, but he maintains that Legree can really do no more to him than kill him and that Christ's promise of redemption will be fulfilled after death. The believer cannot lose, and Cassy wants desperately to believe. She tells Tom the story of her life as the pampered daughter of a slave owner who, like Augustine St. Clare, had meant to free her but had died suddenly before doing so. Cassy's sordid tale of the betrayal of love and the loss of her children is horribly fascinating—and is an increasingly familiar plight in the novel. Cassy is half-mad with despair, and Tom is her last hope.

In **chapter thirty-five** we witness the intensely superstitious nature of Simon Legree. Presented with a coin and a lock of hair found in a packet tied around Tom's neck when he was flogged, Legree thinks of his kindhearted mother, whom he abandoned to pursue the "boisterous, unruly, and tyrannical" ways of his father. Haunted by this reminder, he burns the lock of hair, which Tom received from Eva before her death, and hurls the coin through a window. Cassy warns Legree to leave Tom alone or he will lose time and money harvesting the cotton (**chapter thirty-six**). Legree, who attempts to force an apology out of Tom without success, vows to exact punishment after the harvest.

Chapter thirty-seven briefly returns to the story of George and Eliza Harris as they reach Canada. The exhilaration of their journey to freedom is mirrored in the renewed hope of liberty that Tom eventually inspires in Cassy. In **chapter thirty-eight**, Tom calms Cassy with his gentle and steadfast spirituality. He observes that, while he has the strength to endure his present servitude, Cassy no longer does. She plans a surprisingly simple escape for herself and Emmeline, whom she has befriended (**chapter thirty-nine**).

The garret of Legree's plantation house is believed haunted since the mysterious death of a slave woman there years ago. Cassy subtly revives and intensifies this belief in the imaginations of the slaves and Legree. So when she and Emmeline disappear, everyone believes that they have either escaped or have perished in the swamp, and the noises heard in the garret, where the two are actually hiding, only confirm belief in the ghosts. From her hiding place Cassy witnesses the martyrdom of Tom (**chapter forty**). He refuses to reveal what he knows of the women's disappearance and is beaten severely by Legree and two slaves who have been made, by manipulation and abuse, to betray and torment their fellow slaves. The "savage men" repent, weeping and asking Tom to tell them about Jesus. Christ-like, Tom forgives them.

In **chapter forty-one** young George Shelby, having received Ophelia's letter, at last locates Tom and intends to buy him back in fulfillment of his promise. He arrives too late to save him, but not too late to comfort his old friend at his death. Tom counsels forgiveness as he dies, and even Legree seems momentarily awed by his persistent faith and his saintliness. George vows to God that he will do everything he can to "drive out this curse of slavery." That night Cassy and Emmeline leave the plantation, and slaves will later speak of having seen two white figures "gliding" upon the road (**chapter forty-two**). Disguised as a Creole woman and her servant, they board a riverboat headed north.

In the same chapter we learn of a string of coincidences uniting many of the novel's characters in familial relationships long severed by slavery. A woman on the boat reveals the existence of Cassy's long-lost daughter—who, we learn, is Eliza (**chapter forty-three**). The woman, whose master had freed her, married her, and left her a fortune upon his death, is George Harris's sister. All are reunited in Canada, where the Harris household becomes a place of education, refinement, and family love.

In **chapter forty-four** Chloe and the Shelbys learn of Tom's death from George Shelby. Now the master of his father's plantation, George frees all the slaves, promising them fair wages should they decide to stay on. He attributes his change of heart to the courageous life and brutal death of Tom.

As the extended family of George Harris makes plans to emigrate to Liberia, the reader senses the author's perplexity over the future of race relations in a Christian democracy that has yet to abolish slavery. Through the character of George, Stowe suggests that the hope for true freedom may be possible only in another country. "[W]hat can I do for [my enslaved brethren] here?" George asks, in a letter to a friend. "[L]et me go and form part of a nation, which shall have a voice in the councils of nations, and then we can speak." He continues:

> We *ought* to be free to . . . rise by our individual worth . . . and they who deny us this right are false to their own professed principles of human equality. . . . We have *more* than the rights of common men;—we have the claim of an injured race for reparation. But, then, *I do not want it;* I want a country, a nation, of my own.

In **chapter forty-five** Stowe asserts in her own voice that many of the characters and incidents in the novel are based on actual people and occurrences. She acknowledges the troubling responsibility that will arise with the end of slavery: "Does not every American Christian owe to the African race some effort at reparation for the wrongs that the American nation has brought upon them?" Skeptical that justice to former slaves is possible in a nation in which the slave trade is firmly entrenched, Stowe suggests that the best way to make amends is to assure that the emancipated slave is provided an education before returning to Africa. She concludes with a resounding call to "repentance, justice and mercy" on the part of both Northern and Southern Americans, invoking the "wrath of Almighty God" on those who will not heed this call to save the Union.

Despite its melodramatic style, *Uncle Tom's Cabin* is an immensely moving novel and a social document of American culture. Harriet Beecher Stowe struggles, not altogether unconsciously, against her own racism as she attacks, with passion, a truly evil institution. By appealing to sentiment, evoking an emotional identification with the slave, and counseling a more Christ-like interpretation of Scripture, Stowe may convince the modern reader that, if slavery was not the issue that caused the Civil War, it should have been. ✣

—Tenley Williams
New York University

List of Characters

Uncle Tom, a slave, is a figure of Christ-like suffering and endurance. He is a loving husband and father, an honorable man in a dishonorable society. A model of passive resistance, he draws his strength from his unquestioning faith in the Christian promise of a better life to come. For Tom, the present is explicable only as a part of God's greater vision, so he patiently accepts the misery of his life and the lives of the slaves around him, without hope of social reform. His religious strength comforts those who suffer as it awakens in his oppressors a recognition of God's mercy and a fear of his retribution. He dies a martyr's death, refusing to betray two escaped slaves.

George and Eliza, although slaves on separate plantations, marry and have a son. The family stays together only through the clemency and the financial stability of their masters, and when Eliza learns that her son is to be sold, she flees north. George is reunited with the family, and they eventually establish a home in Canada. The desire for political dialogue and power ultimately motivates George to move his family to Liberia, a new African nation with modern ideals.

Evangeline St. Clare—"Little Eva"—is the precocious daughter of a slave owner. A kindred soul to Tom, she is a figure of spiritual purity. Like Tom, she believes that Christ will deliver all into a better life after death and that the task of both slaves and slave owners is to work to earn this reward. Eva dies of consumption, and her exemplary life motivates all who know her to emulate her kindness and compassion.

Augustine St. Clare is a slave owner whose beliefs are poised between the Northern and Southern viewpoints. He understands both the pretensions of abolitionist ideality and the cancerous corruption of slavery in the plantation system. He is kind and generous to his slaves and is both bemused and spiritually overwhelmed by his power over their lives. His self-confessed flaw is his laziness, and St. Clare's weakness of character costs his slaves their freedom, and, in Tom's case, his life: St. Clare dies before implementing his promise to emancipate him.

Ophelia St. Clare is Augustine's cousin, brought from Vermont to oversee his household and the care of Eva. She is an organized, well-read, sensible abolitionist who is nonetheless repulsed by the thought of touching a "Negro." Through Eva's example of racially blind love, she experiences an epiphany at Eva's death that inspires in her a capacity to love her young charge, Topsy.

Marie St. Clare, the mother of Little Eva, is a self-absorbed hypochondriac incapable either of loving or of being loved, though Eva tries. She is irredeemably racist, and—by ignoring her husband's final wish to emancipate him—she proves instrumental in Tom's doom.

Topsy, a slave girl, is the most startling and arguably the most charming character in the novel. Raised as though she were livestock, she has never known parents, family, or love, yet Topsy is as pure of heart as Little Eva. St. Clare purchases Topsy for Ophelia, challenging her to practice her Northern moral precepts and spiritual pretensions with a child who has known nothing of God or of family life. She is acutely aware of Ophelia's disgust at her touch and articulates her perceptions without equivocating. She and Little Eva become friends and, after Eva's death, Topsy's inherent goodness wins Ophelia's love.

Simon Legree is the corrupt and brutal plantation owner who buys Tom after the death of Augustine St. Clare. A spiritually barren man, he is ruled by his appetites and superstitions. Through him Stowe alludes to the sexual servitude of young slave women and girls in the figures of the tragically betrayed Cassy and the morally imperiled Emmeline. Legree beats Tom to death.

Cassy is the slave mistress of Simon Legree, sent to work the fields when he replaces her with Emmeline, a young girl purchased at auction. The daughter of a slave mother and a wealthy and loving slave holder who meant to free her legally, the once-beautiful Cassy is refined and graceful. Alternately embraced by the white world and abandoned to slavery, she had lived a life of privilege with a white master in whose love she had trusted. But he abandoned her and their children, selling them all into slavery, and Cassy is filled with despair. She is drawn to Tom because of his spiritual strength. His stoic endurance restores Cassy's hope, and with Emmeline she escapes to Canada and is reunited with her long-lost daughter Eliza. ✤

Critical Views

HARRIET BEECHER STOWE ON THE SOURCES FOR THE
CHARACTER OF UNCLE TOM

[*Uncle Tom's Cabin* was violently attacked by many different parties and for a variety of reasons; one of the criticisms concerned the seeming unreality of the characters. In *A Key to* Uncle Tom's Cabin (1853), Stowe defends the book and, in the following excerpt, maintains that the character of Uncle Tom was drawn from several black slaves she knew personally.]

The character of Uncle Tom has been objected to as improbable; and yet the writer has received more confirmations of that character, and from a great variety of sources, than of any other in the book.

Many people have said to her, "I knew an Uncle Tom in such-and-such a Southern State." All the histories of this kind which have thus been related to her would of themselves, if collected, make a small volume. The author will relate a few of them.

While visiting in an obscure town in Maine, in the family of a friend, the conversation happened to turn upon this subject, and the gentleman with whose family she was staying related the following. He said, that when on a visit to his brother in New Orleans, some years before, he found in his possession a most valuable negro man, of such remarkable probity and honesty that his brother literally trusted him with all he had. He had frequently seen him take out a handful of bills, without looking at them, and hand them to this servant, bidding him go and provide what was necessary for the family, and bring him the change. He remonstrated with his brother on this imprudence; but the latter replied that he had had such proofs of this servant's impregnable conscientiousness that he felt it safe to trust him to any extent.

The history of the servant was this. He had belonged to a man in Baltimore, who, having a general prejudice against all the religious exercises of slaves, did all that he could to prevent his having any time for devotional duties, and strictly forbade him to read the Bible and pray, either by himself or with the other servants; and because, like a certain man of old, named Daniel, he constantly disobeyed this unchristian edict, his master inflicted upon him that punishment which a master always has in his power to inflict—he sold him into perpetual exile from his wife and children, down to New Orleans.

The gentleman who gave the writer this information says that, although not a religious man at the time, he was so struck with the man's piety, that he said to his brother, "I hope you will never do anything to deprive this man of his religious privileges, for I think a judgment will come upon you if you do." To this his brother replied that he should be very foolish to do it, since he had made up his mind that the man's religion was the root of his extraordinary excellences. ⟨. . .⟩

In the town of Brunswick, Maine, where the writer lived when writing *Uncle Tom's Cabin,* may now be seen the grave of an aged coloured woman, named Phebe, who was so eminent for her piety and loveliness of character, that the writer has never heard her name mentioned except with that degree of awe and respect which one would imagine due to a saint. The small cottage where she resided is still visited and looked upon as a sort of shrine, as the spot where old Phebe lived and prayed. Her prayers and pious exhortations were supposed to have been the cause of the conversion of many young people in the place. Notwithstanding that the unchristian feeling of caste prevails as strongly in Maine as anywhere else in New England, and the negro, commonly speaking, is an object of aversion and contempt, yet so great was the influence of her piety and loveliness of character, that she was uniformly treated with the utmost respect and attention by all classes of people. The most cultivated and intelligent ladies of the place esteemed it a privilege to visit her cottage; and when she was old and helpless, her wants were most tenderly provided for. When the news of her death was spread abroad in the place, it excited a general and very tender sensation of regret. "We have lost Phebe's prayers," was the remark frequently made afterwards by members of the church, as they met one another. At her funeral, the ex-governor of the State and the professors of the college officiated as pall-bearers, and a sermon was preached, in which the many excellences of her Christian character were held up as an example to the community. A small religious tract, containing an account of her life, was published by the American Tract Society, prepared by a lady of Brunswick. The writer recollects that on reading the tract, when she first went to Brunswick, a doubt arose in her mind whether it was not somewhat exaggerated. Some time afterwards she overheard some young persons conversing together about the tract, and saying that they did not think it gave exactly the right idea of Phebe. "Why, is it too highly coloured?" was the inquiry of the author. "Oh, no, no, indeed!" was the earnest response; "it doesn't begin to give an idea of how good she was."

Such instances as these serve to illustrate the words of the Apostle, "God hath chosen the foolish things of the world to confound the wise; and God hath chosen the weak things of the world to confound the things which are mighty."

—Harriet Beecher Stowe, *A Key to* Uncle Tom's Cabin (1853; rev. ed. Boston: John P. Jewett Co., 1854), pp. 37–38, 40–41

SAMUEL WARREN ON *UNCLE TOM'S CABIN* AS AN AGENT OF SOCIAL CHANGE

[Samuel Warren (1807–1877), a British novelist, critic, and physician, wrote a number of technical legal works, many reviews, and several novels. In this review of *Uncle Tom's Cabin,* Warren praises the authenticity of the work but questions whether it will have any actual effect as a political tract.]

Uncle Tom's Cabin is a remarkable book unquestionably; and, upon the whole, we are not surprised at its prodigious success, even as a mere literary performance; but whether, after all, it will have any direct effect upon the dreadful INSTITUTION at which it is aimed, may be regarded as problematical. Of one thing we are persuaded—that its author, as she has displayed in this work undoubted genius, in some respects of a higher order than any American predecessor or contemporary, is also a woman of unaffected and profound piety, and an ardent friend of the unhappy black. Every word in her pages issues glistening and warm from the mint of woman's love and sympathy, refined and purified by Christianity. We never saw in any other work, so many and such sudden irresistible appeals to the reader's heart—appeals which, moreover, only a wife and a mother could make. One's heart throbs, and one's eyes are suffused with tears without a moment's notice, and without anything like effort or preparation on the writer's part. We are, on the contrary, soothed in our spontaneous emotion by a conviction of the writer's utter artlessness; and when once a gifted woman has satisfied her most captious reader that such is the case, she thenceforth leads him on, with an air of loving and tender triumph, a willing captive to the last. There are, indeed, scenes and touches in this book which no living writer, that we know of, can surpass, and perhaps none even equal.

No English man or woman, again, could have written it—no one, but an actual spectator of the scenes described, or one whose life is spent with those moving among them; scenes scarce appreciable by FREE English readers—fathers, mothers, husbands, wives, brothers and sisters. We can hardly *realise* to ourselves human nature tried so tremendously as, It seems, Is only adumbrated in these pages. An Englishman's soul swells at the bare idea of such submission to the tyrannous will of man over his fellowman, as the reader of this volume becomes grievously familiar with; and yet we are assured by Mrs Stowe that she has given us only occasional glimpses of the indescribable horrors of slavery. To this part of the subject, however, we shall return. Let us speak first, and In only general terms, of the literary characteristics of the author, as displayed in her work.

Mrs Stowe is unquestionably a woman of GENIUS; and that is a word which we always use charily: regarding genius as a thing *per se*—different from talent, in its highest development, altogether, and in kind. Quickness, shrewdness, energy, intensity, may, and frequently do accompany, but do not constitute genius. Its divine spark is the direct and special gift of God: we cannot completely analyse it, though we may detect its presence, and the nature of many of its attributes, by its action; and the skill of higher criticism is requisite, in order to distinguish between the feats of genius and the operations of talent. Now, we imagine that no person of genius can read *Uncle Tom's Cabin,* and not feel in glowing contact with genius—generally gentle and tender, but capable of rising, with its theme, into very high regions of dramatic power. This Mrs Stowe has done several times in the work before us—exhibiting a passion, an intensity, a subtle delicacy of perception, a melting tenderness, which are as far out of the reach of mere talent, however well trained and experienced, as the prismatic colours are out of the reach of the born blind. But the genius of Mrs Stowe is of that kind which instinctively addresses itself to the Affections; and though most at home with the gentler, it can be yet fearlessly familiar with the fiercest passions which can agitate and rend the human breast. With the one she can exhibit an exquisite tenderness and sympathy; watching the other, however, with stern but calm scrutiny, and delineating both with a truth and simplicity, in the one case touching, in the other really *terrible.*

"*Free* men of the North, and Christians," says she, in her own vigorous and earnest way, "cannot know *what slavery is.* . . . From this arose a desire," on the author's part, "to exhibit it in a *living dramatic reality.* She has endeavoured to show it fairly in its best and its worst phases. In its *best* aspect, she has perhaps been successful; but oh! who shall say what yet remains untold in that *valley and shadow of death* that lies on the other side? . . . . The writer has only given a faint shadow—a dim picture—of the anguish and despair that are at this very moment riving thousands of hearts, shattering thousands of families, and driving a helpless and sensitive race to frenzy and despair."

—Samuel Warren, [Review of Uncle Tom's Cabin], Blackwood's Edinburgh Magazine No. 456 (October 1853): 395–96

J. W. DeForest on the Search for the Great American Novel

[J. W. DeForest (1826–1906), a historian and novelist, is the author of *History of the Indians of Connecticut* (1853) and *Miss Ravenel's Conversion from Secession to Loyalty* (1867), a Civil War novel. In this extract, DeForest argues that *Uncle Tom's Cabin,* despite its flaws, could be classified as the closest approximation to the "great American novel" because of its breadth of purpose and depth of feeling.]

The nearest approach to the desired phenomenon "the great American novel" is *Uncle Tom's Cabin.* There were very noticeable faults in that story; there was a very faulty plot; there was (if idealism be a fault) a black man painted whiter than the angels, and a girl such as girls are to be, perhaps, but are not yet; there was a little village twaddle. But there was also a national breadth to the picture, truthful outlining of character, natural speaking, and plenty of strong feeling. Though comeliness of form was lacking, the material of the work was in many respects admirable. Such Northerners as Mrs. Stowe painted we have seen; and we have seen such Southerners, no matter what the people south of Mason and Dixon's line may protest; we have seen such negroes, barring, of course, the impeccable Uncle Tom—uncle of no extant nephews, so far as we know. It was a picture of American life, drawn with a few strong and passionate strokes, not filled in thoroughly, but still a portrait.
—J. W. DeForest, "The Great American Novel," *Nation,* 9 January 1868, p. 28

Charles F. Richardson on Some Reasons for the Success of *Uncle Tom's Cabin*

[Charles F. Richardson (1851–1913) wrote *The Choice of Books* (1900) and *American Literature 1607–1885*

(1887–89), from which the following extract is taken. Here, Richardson argues that the success of *Uncle Tom's Cabin* rests on Stowe's ability to create sympathetic and realistic characters and on her willingness to leaven her serious intent and melodramatic style with passages of humor.]

In the far cold North, where her husband was at the time a professor in Bowdoin College, Mrs. Stowe looked toward the sunlit South, and beheld beneath fair skies all the horror of the wide-spread and blighting evil of human slavery, with its curses of lust and lash, broken homes and bleeding hearts; hate and cruelty and greed on the one hand, and the dogged endurance of hopeless woe on the other. The horrible system of slavery was not unmitigated by occasional kindness; many a freedman has sincerely said that sorrow and suffering never came until abolition severed him from the old master and mistress, and threw him all unfit upon the world, with a ballot in his hand but no wisdom in his brain. Yet no question of past political expediency, no consideration, even, of exaggeration in the book, as regards the average condition of the negroes in the Southern States, can blind our eyes to the essential and enduring success of the novel. It is far from faultless in development of plot, delineation of character, or literary style; but it strongly seizes a significant theme, treats it with immediate originality and inevitable effect, and meanwhile adds several individual characters to the gallery of fiction. It was everywhere an anti-slavery argument because its pictures of episodes in the history of slavery were so manifest and so thrilling. Read in every state of the North and in parts of the South, and translated into twenty languages of Europe, it aroused the indifferent and quickened the philanthropic. Its power was felt, perhaps unconsciously, before a quarter of its pages had been read.

The author of "Uncle Tom's Cabin" had the wisdom—not possessed by the pessimistic or self-blinded delineators of later woes in Russia—to brighten her pages by touches of humor and kindly humanity, and to obey the canons of the novelist's art as well as those of the moralist's conscience. Thereby her force was quadrupled, for literature both popularizes and perpetuates morality, while morality without art is fatal to literature. The book remains a vivid panorama of people and scene in a bygone time, now remanded by final war to a past that must ever be historic and can never be repeated. The "abolition of tribal relations in Christ" was the broad theme of a Christian woman; and in treating it she produced an art-result of such inherent merit that the hand helped the soul as much as the soul the hand.

—Charles F. Richardson, *American Literature 1607–1885* (New York: Putnam's, 1887–89), Vol. 2, pp. 410–12

CHARLES EDWARD STOWE ON SOME TRUE INCIDENTS BEHIND STOWE'S FICTION

[Charles Edward Stowe (b. 1850), the son of Harriet Beecher Stowe, compiled an important biography of his mother from her journals and letters (1889). In an extract from that work, Stowe tells how an actual incident involving an escaped slave led in part to the writing of *Uncle Tom's Cabin*.]

In 1839 Mrs. Stowe received into her family as a servant a colored girl from Kentucky. By the laws of Ohio she was free, having been brought into the State and left there by her mistress. In spite of this, Professor Stowe received word, after she had lived with them some months, that the girl's master was in the city looking for her, and that if she were not careful she would be seized and conveyed back into slavery. Finding that this could be accomplished by boldness, perjury, and the connivance of some unscrupulous justice, Professor Stowe determined to remove the girl to some place of security where she might remain until the search for her should be given up. Accordingly he and his brother-in-law, Henry Ward Beecher, both armed, drove the fugitive, in a covered wagon, at night, by unfrequented roads, twelve miles back into the country, and left her in safety with the family of old John Van Zandt, the fugitive's friend.

It is from this incident of real life and personal experience that Mrs. Stowe conceived the thrilling episode of the fugitives' escape from Tom Loker and Marks In *Uncle Tom's Cabin.*

—Charles Edward Stowe, *Life of Harriet Beecher Stowe Compiled from Her Letters* (Boston: Houghton, Mifflin, 1889), p. 93

BRANDER MATTHEWS ON STOWE'S FAIRNESS

[Brander Matthews (1852–1929) was an important American critic, editor, and novelist. He wrote many volumes, including *An Introduction to the Study of American Literature* (1896) and *The Development of the Drama* (1903). In this extract, Matthews comments that Stowe was fair in her portrayal of Southerners, since she blamed the institution of slavery and not individuals.]

The smoke of the war has cleared away now and the heat of combat has died down; and as one reads the book with unimpassioned eye, it is easy to understand why Mrs. Stowe thought that she had dealt so fairly with the southern people that they would not be offended. As we read it now we see that the indictment of the system was so damning that those who accepted slavery could not but denounce the book and declare it detestable. While proving that slavery itself was black and foul and hideous, the authoress was perfectly fair to the slaveholders themselves, showing that it was the system which was bad and not the individual. The most offensive, brutal, hardened character in the book is Simon Legree—and he is a New Englander. The pleasantest and most welcome character in the book is St. Clare—and he is a native southerner: indeed it may be questioned whether the new southern novelists, skilful as they are and understanding their fellow southerners as they do, have as yet given us any portrait of the southern gentleman as charming as Mrs. Stowe's St. Clare, as easy, as good-humored, as quick-witted, as kindly, as keen, as lazy, or as true to life itself. The contrast between St. Clare and Legree forces itself on every reader, however careless; and with a due sense of climax the dark figure comes last.

Even the careless reader today will see that the story straggles not a little and lacks firm structure; it bears evidence that it was written from week to week, without a settled plan, and that it grew on the author's hands almost in spite of herself. As Mrs. Stowe told the publisher, "the story made itself, and that she could not stop till it was done." The tale was nearly half told before the need for "comedy relief," as the playmakers phrase it, led to the introduction of Topsy, perhaps the most popular figure in the book; and it was drawing to its close before we were made acquainted with Cassy, perhaps the most picturesque character in the story and certainly not the least true. The intensity of the author's feeling was so keen, her knowledge of her subject was so wide, her unconscious and intuitive artistic impulse was so vigorous, that she shaped her story so as best to accomplish its purpose, building better than she knew and doing more than she dared to hope.

—Brander Matthews, "American Fiction Again," Cosmopolitan
13, No. 3 (March 1892): 637

Thomas Wentworth Higginson on Some Criticisms of Uncle Tom's Cabin

[Thomas Wentworth Higginson (1823–1911), an important American critic, is the author of *Short Studies of American Authors* (1880), *Hints on Writing and Speech-Making* (1898), and *Contemporaries* (1899). He was the first editor of the poems of Emily Dickinson (1891). In this extract, Higginson takes note of some criticisms, especially from Southerners, of *Uncle Tom's Cabin.*]

A further question has sometimes been raised as to how far the book was correct in its pictures of slavery. One result of this debate was to induce Mrs. Stowe to publish, in 1853, a *Key to* Uncle Tom's Cabin, giving chapter and verse, so to speak, for every incident she had employed. It is certain that many

Southerners of high standing, beginning with Senator Preston of South Carolina—in a conversation with Prof. Lieber—admitted that every fact it contained might be duplicated from their own observation. All this might be true, however, and yet the general atmosphere of such a book might be unfair; there might be unfairness also in the omissions. It is stated by Mrs. Stowe herself that she expected more criticism from the abolitionists than from the slaveholders themselves. Perhaps the keenest criticism ever made upon *Uncle Tom's Cabin* was from a Southern lady who, while conceding the probable truth of all the incidents, complained that Mrs. Stowe had described neither the best nor the worst class of slaveholders. Those who could not accept Legree as a sufficient approach to the latter type must have had a terrible experience. As to the former, it is enough to say that Mrs. Stowe was consciously engaged upon an anti-slavery tract, not, like Frederick Law Olmsted, in an economic study; and that the very impotence of the more humane slaveholders either to emancipate their slaves or to extricate themselves from the toils of the system, is not the least weighty part of the indictment against American slavery.

—Thomas Wentworth Higginson, "Harriet Beecher Stowe," *Nation*, 9 July 1896, p. 25

FRED LEWIS PATTEE ON STOWE AND DICKENS

[Fred Lewis Pattee (1863–1950) was a prominent scholar of American literature. He wrote *Side Lights on American Literature* (1922), *The Development of the American Short Story* (1923), and *The First Century of American Literature 1770–1870* (1935). In this extract, Pattee likens the techniques used by Stowe to make an argument for social change to the techniques used by Charles Dickens, maintaining that both writers appealed chiefly to the emotions rather than to the intellect.]

Her attack upon slavery was not obvious. She did not preach and she did not argue and she made no frontal attack. Like

Dickens, she aroused emotion; she created characters that her reader could feel as if they were present in the room. The victims were under-dogs, and in America they were therefore to be pitied. The oppressors were all utter villains. The novel came in the one moment in history when it would have been received as a world classic. For America was tense with emotion, and that emotion was almost as intense in Europe, especially in England. As a period novel it had every element that would make for popularity: it was melodramatic, with a hero and heroines and villains; it was sentimental even to the Dickens extremes; it had humor of the Jim Crow type; it had negro spirituals sung by slaves; and it had a strong religious motif such as could come only from one reared, as she had been, in such an atmosphere as she was later to present in her *Oldtown Folks.*

Dickens with his *Pickwick* and his *Oliver Twist* and the novels that followed undoubtedly created a new reading public. Hostlers and weavers and servant girls who never before had thought of books as things to be read laughed over Sam Weller and the fat boy and cried when Paul Dombey died and Little Nell. In the same way *Uncle Tom's Cabin* enlarged greatly the American reading public. For one thing it broke down a long stretch of the stockade that had guarded Puritan families from the "contagion" of novels, long believed in Christian homes to be works inspired by the devil. Everybody read *Uncle Tom.* Was it not history? Was it not a weapon against slavery? Was not Mrs. Stowe saying that the hand of God held her hand as she wrote it? And they followed it into the theater and saw Little Eva go up to Heaven on a wire which they did not see, with "not a dry eye in the house." They saw Eliza cross the ice with her baby in her arms and the awful bloodhounds leaping at her throat, and they went home shuddering at the death of Uncle Tom ready to canonize him as a veritable saint. Surely uncounted thousands went to see a Tom drama who never before had seen the inside of a theater.

—Fred Lewis Pattee, *The Feminine Fifties* (New York: D. Appleton-Century, 1940), pp. 137–38

[James Baldwin (1924–1987), an important black American novelist, was also an occasional critic. Among his works of nonfiction are *Notes of a Native Son* (1955), *Nobody Knows My Name* (1961), and *The Evidence of Things Not Seen* (1985). In this extract from his celebrated essay on *Uncle Tom's Cabin*, Baldwin argues that Stowe's work is not so much a novel as an abolitionist tract and that it is a failure as a work of fiction.]

Uncle Tom's Cabin is a very bad novel, having, in its self-righteous, virtuous sentimentality, much in common with *Little Women.* Sentimentality, the ostentatious parading of excessive and spurious emotion, is the mark of dishonesty, the inability to feel; the wet eyes of the sentimentalist betray his aversion to experience, his fear of life, his arid heart; and it is always, therefore, the signal of secret and violent inhumanity, the mask of cruelty. *Uncle Tom's Cabin*—like its multitudinous, hard-boiled descendants—is a catalogue of violence. This is explained by the nature of Mrs. Stowe's subject matter, her laudable determination to flinch from nothing in presenting the complete picture; an explanation which falters only if we pause to ask whether or not her picture is indeed complete; and what constriction or failure of perception forced her to do so depend on the description of brutality—unmotivated, senseless—and to leave unanswered and unnoticed the only important question: what it was, after all, that moved her people to such deeds.

But this, let us say, was beyond Mrs. Stowe's powers; she was not so much a novelist as an impassioned pamphleteer; her book was not intended to do anything more than prove that slavery was wrong; was, in fact, perfectly horrible. This makes material for a pamphlet but it is hardly enough for a novel; and the only question left to ask is why we are bound still within the same constriction. How is it that we are so loath to make a further journey than that made by Mrs. Stowe, to discover and reveal something a little closer to the truth?

⟨. . .⟩ The figure from whom the novel takes its name, Uncle Tom, who is a figure of controversy yet, is jet-black, wooly-haired, illiterate; and he is phenomenally forbearing. He has to be; he is black; only through this forbearance can he survive or triumph. (Cf. Faulkner's preface to *The Sound and the Fury:* These others were not Compsons. They were black:—They endured.) His triumph is metaphysical, unearthly; since he is black, born without the light, it is only through humility, the incessant mortification of the flesh, that he can enter into communion with God or man. The virtuous rage of Mrs. Stowe is motivated by nothing so temporal as a concern for the relationship of men to one another—or, even, as she would have claimed, by a concern for their relationship to God—but merely by a panic of being hurled into the flames, of being caught in traffic with the devil. She embraced this merciless doctrine with all her heart, bargaining shamelessly before the throne of grace: God and salvation becoming her personal property, purchased with the coin of her virtue. Here, black equates with evil and white with grace; if, being mindful of the necessity of good works, she could not cast out the blacks—a wretched, huddled mass, apparently, claiming, like an obsession, her inner eye—she could not embrace them either without purifying them of sin. She must cover their intimidating nakedness, robe them in white, the garments of salvation; only thus could she herself be delivered from ever-present sin, only thus could she bury, as St. Paul demanded, "the carnal man, the man of the flesh." Tom, therefore, her only black man, has been robbed of his humanity and divested of his sex. It is the price for that darkness with which he has been branded.

—James Baldwin, "Everybody's Protest Novel," *Partisan Review* 16, No. 6 (June 1949): 578–79, 581

CHARLES H. FOSTER ON THE MERITS OF *UNCLE TOM'S CABIN*

[Charles H. Foster (b. 1913) taught at the University of Iowa, Grinnell College, and the University of Minnesota. He has edited *Emerson's Theory of Poetry* (1939) and *The Rungless Ladder* (1954), a book on Stowe from which the following extract is taken. Here, ιoster ponders the merits of Stowe's novel: It bears relations with the work of James Fenimore Cooper and Mark Twain and anticipates later fiction by southerners, especially William Faulkner.]

Uncle Tom's Cabin belongs to a lower species than the American masterworks of the 1850's: The Scarlet Letter, Moby-Dick, Walden, and Leaves of Grass. As writer, Harriet stands close to that other important regional novelist, James Fenimore Cooper, who died the year before Uncle Tom's Cabin appeared as a book. Like Cooper, she did not see her way to the destruction of the conventional novel and the creation of a new form appropriate to her new subject matter. Like him, she continued in broad outlines the tradition of the sentimental novel. George and Eliza have much of the rhetorical unreality of similar characters in Cooper and, if we remember the incident of the slave catchers, they are even involved in an approximation of Cooperesque flight and pursuit with the woodsman in the form of Phineas Fletcher thrown in for good measure. But much more significant is the similarity between Uncle Tom's Cabin and The Pioneers, for example, in their true centers of interest. In Natty Bumppo and Uncle Tom, Harriet and Cooper were not seeking to create myth; they were simply projecting against the American landscape figures larger than life who stalked their imaginations. Something closely resembling myth resulted, however, in both instances. As Natty Bumppo popularly became the archetypal frontiersman ever in conflict with civilization, so Uncle Tom became the archetypal American Negro, exploited by the white man and sold South symbolically again and again. Uncle Tom is still a figure who can move us as we read. In our concentration on the truly artistic mythmaker, Melville, we are likely to underrate Harriet's achievement. Criticism must eventually recognize her, I believe, as a major mythmaker to the populace throughout the world.

Once we grant the importance of Uncle Tom as myth is there any other aspect of Harriet's first novel which may hold our attention on the literary level? Uncle Tom appears overidealized when we compare him with Jim in Huckleberry Finn, and Lucy and Cassy fare only slightly better when we compare them with Roxana in Pudd'nhead Wilson. But, as I have indicated, Sam, Marks, and Dinah would not be out of place in

Mark Twain's St. Petersburg and Dawson's Landing. These characters, together with Miss Ophelia and her Vermont friends and relations, by fits and starts bring us into a vigorously conceived American world.

It is possible also that some readers of fiction will be intrigued by Harriet's anticipation of Faulkner, Caldwell, and other contemporary Southern writers. Faulkner's objective correlative to his awareness of the curse brought to the South by slavery is one of the major works of the American imagination. Harriet's St. Clare family appears paper-thin by comparison; but the Sutpens, the Sartorises, the Compsons are more clearly implied in Alfred St. Clare, his son Henrique, and Augustine's wife, Marie, than in characters of any earlier American book. Perhaps the most striking foreshadowing of Faulkner is the denouement of the novel. In terms of his legend, as it is brought down to modern times, there is something almost prophetic in the fact that Uncle Tom, the Negro, who was not freed by his noble but ineffective master, becomes the property of a man embodying the greed, the vulgarity, the lust, the inhumanity which outrage Faulkner as he broods over the South following the heroic days.

—Charles H. Foster, *The Rungless Ladder: Harriet Beecher Stowe and New England Puritanism* (Durham, NC: Duke University Press, 1954), pp. 59–61

EDMUND WILSON ON THE "ERUPTIVE FORCE" OF *UNCLE TOM'S CABIN*

[Edmund Wilson (1895–1972) was perhaps the leading American literary critic of his age. Among his many works are *The Wound and the Bow* (1947), *Axel's Castle: A Study in the Imaginative Literature of 1870–1930* (1931), and *Patriotic Gore* (1962), a landmark work on Civil War literature from which the following extract is taken. Here, Wilson claims that Stowe's novel has not received the attention it deserves and goes on to praise its "eruptive force" and skillful characterization.]

To expose oneself in maturity to *Uncle Tom* may therefore prove a startling experience. It is a much more impressive work than one has ever been allowed to suspect. The first thing that strikes one about it is a certain eruptive force. This is partly explained by the author in a preface to a late edition, in which she tells of the oppressive silence that hung over the whole question of slavery before she published her book. "It was a general saying," she explains, "among conservative and saga-cious people that this subject was a dangerous one to investi-gate, and that nobody could begin to read and think upon it without becoming practically insane; moreover, that it was a subject of such delicacy that no discussion of it could be held in the free states without impinging upon the sensibilities of the slave states, to whom alone the management of the matter belonged." The story came so suddenly to Mrs. Stowe and seemed so irresistibly to write itself that she felt as if some power beyond her had laid hold of her to deliver its message, and she said sometimes that the book had been written by God. This is actually a little the impression that the novel makes on the reader. Out of a background of undistinguished narra-tive, inelegantly and carelessly written, the characters leap into being with a vitality that is all the more striking for the inepti-tude of the prose that presents them. These characters—like those of Dickens, at least in his early phase—express them-selves a good deal better than the author expresses herself. The Shelbys and George Harris and Eliza and Aunt Chloe and Uncle Tom project themselves out of the void. They come before us arguing and struggling, like real people who cannot be quiet. We feel that the dams of discretion of which Mrs. Stowe has spoken have been burst by a passionate force that, compressed, has been mounting behind them, and which, lib-erated, has taken the form of a flock of lamenting and ranting, prattling and preaching characters, in a drama that demands to be played to the end.

Not, however, that it is merely a question of a troubled imag-ination and an inhibited emotional impulse finding vent in a waking fantasy. What is most unexpected is that, the farther one reads in *Uncle Tom,* the more one becomes aware that a critical mind is at work, which has the complex situation in a very firm grip and which, no matter how vehement the characters become, is controlling and coördinating their interrelations. Though there is much that is exciting in *Uncle Tom's Cabin,* it is never the crude melodrama of the decadent phase of the play; and though we find some old-fashioned moralizing and a couple of Dickensian deathbeds, there is a good deal less sentimentality than we may have been prepared for by our memories of the once celebrated stage apotheosis—if we are old enough to have seen it: "Little Eva in the Realms of Gold." We may even be surprised to discover that the novel is by no means an indictment drawn up by New England against the South. Mrs. Stowe has, on the contrary, been careful to contrive her story in such a way that the Southern states and New England shall be shown as involved to an equal degree in the kidnapping into slavery of the Negroes and the subsequent maltreatment of them, and that the emphasis shall all be laid on the impracticability of slavery as a permanent institution. The author, if anything, leans over backwards in trying to make it plain that the New Englanders are as much to blame as the South and to exhibit the Southerners in a favorable light ⟨. . .⟩

—Edmund Wilson, "Harriet Beecher Stowe," *Patriotic Gore: Studies in the Literature of the American Civil War* (New York: Oxford University Press, 1962), pp. 5–7

ALICE C. CROZIER ON *UNCLE TOM'S CABIN* AS POLEMIC

[Alice C. Crozier is a professor of English at Rutgers University in New Brunswick, New Jersey. She is the author of *The Novels of Harriet Beecher Stowe* (1969), from which the following extract is taken. Here, Crozier argues that *Uncle Tom's Cabin* is a polemic not so much against the South as against the educated citizens of the North and South who allowed the system of slavery to develop and continue.]

It is no news to anyone that *Uncle Tom's Cabin* is a polemic. Nevertheless, it is useful to clarify the grounds of the argument, and, lest it still be supposed by some that *Uncle Tom's Cabin* is an anti-Southern book, to identify just who is being attacked. This can most readily be done by studying the many references in the novel to the Declaration of Independence and the subjects Mrs. Stowe associates with it. It is also natural to inquire into the remedies, proposed or implied, to which the polemic leads; these are conveyed most clearly through the novel's sentimental heroine, little Eva, and secondarily by the words and example of that "moral miracle," Uncle Tom.

The argument is often introduced by a scene or picture. The strategy is illustrated by one of the scenes on the boat which is taking Uncle Tom from Kentucky to New Orleans. Among the slaves whom Haley has brought and is taking to market is a young woman named Lucy with a baby, whom Haley sells to a man on the boat. The man explains that his " 'cook lost a youn 'un last week,—got drownded in a wash-tub, while she was a hangin' out clothes,—and I reckon it would be well enough to set her to raisin' this yer.' " Haley steals the baby while Lucy is asleep and sells him. Mrs. Stowe expects the reader's wrath to rise at this tale, and she quickly points the moral.

> The trader that arrived at that stage of Christian and political perfection which has been recommended by some preachers and politicians of the north, lately, in which he had completely overcome every humane weakness and prejudice. . . . The wild look of anguish and utter despair that the woman cast on him [when she discovered the sale] might have disturbed one less practised; but he was used to it. He had seen that same look hundreds of times. You can get used to such things, too, my friend; and it is the great object of recent efforts to make our whole northern community used to them, for the glory of the Union.

For the glory of the Union! The ogre, then, is Daniel Webster. Who is to blame? Webster, yes, but also "you" dear reader who allow yourself to rejoice in the glory of the Union.

Mrs. Stowe never makes a point just once. Several pages later, when Haley discovers that the woman has jumped overboard and drowned herself, we are told that Haley's response was

to consider himself an ill-used man, decidedly; but there was no
help for it, as the woman had escaped into a state which *never
will* give up a fugitive,—not even at the demand of the whole
glorious Union. . . .

'He's a shocking creature, isn't he,—this trader? so unfeeling!
It's dreadful, really!'

'O, but nobody thinks anything of these traders! They are uni-
versally despised,—never received into any decent society.'

But who, sir, makes the trader? Who is most to blame? The
enlightened, cultivated, intelligent man, who supports the system of which the trader is the inevitable result, or the poor trader himself? You make the public sentiment that calls for his
trade, that debauches and depraves him, till he feels no shame
in it; and in what are you better than he?

Thus it is the system itself that is evil, and its most corrupt
members are neither the trader nor the slaveholder but rather
the pious, educated, respectable citizenry of North and South
who self-righteously despise the brutish trader but who are too
smug and too selfish to disturb their own complacency on
behalf of reform. The polemic attacks the reader.

—Alice C. Crozier, *The Novels of Harriet Beecher Stowe* (New
York: Oxford University Press, 1969), pp. 7–9

NOEL B. GERSON ON STOWE'S CONCEPTION OF CHRISTIANITY

[Noel B. Gerson (1914–1988) is the author of many
biographies, including those of Pocahontas (1973), the
Marquis de Lafayette (1976), and Harriet Beecher
Stowe (1976), from which the following extract is
taken. Here, Gerson discusses Stowe's conception that
slavery could not exist in a truly Christian world.]

During the long months of writing—and for the rest of her
life—Mrs. Stowe remained convinced she had written a mod-
erate work, consonant with her religion and the teachings of
her father. Her Kentucky family, the Shelbys, were kind and civ-
ilized and treated their slaves with compassion. But they, like
the slaves themselves, were victims of the institution itself, and

it was that institution, its injustices magnified by the cruelties of the cold-blooded, inhumane slave trade, that she sought to expose and destroy.

In a truly Christian world, she believed, slavery could not exist. Its perpetuation was partly the fault of the churches, including the conservative wing of the Presbyterian movement. These organizations had lost sight of two basic tenets: that God's love is all-pervasive and that man redeems himself through Christ. Instead of practicing religion, they had allowed themselves to become enmeshed in hair-splitting theological arguments, while the wicked and the evils they perpetrated flourished.

At no time did the author's common sense desert her. Her slave-owner characters, in the main, are decent, honorable people, themselves victims of the institution of slavery and more commendable than the abolitionists who advocated any means, no matter how violent, to rid the nation of a curse. More radical antislavery elements in the country, she predicted in her correspondence, would be "sorely disappointed" by her book and might even regard her as a traitor to their cause.

She was also concerned with what would become of the former slaves should immediate, complete emancipation be granted. No longer would there be a place for them on the plantations of the South. Illiterate, without the skills that would enable them to work in the factories, they would not be at home in the rapidly industrializing North either, particularly as most Northern citizens, despite their professed antislavery sentiments, were showing no tendency to admit blacks into their homes, their schools, or even their churches. To send all the freed slaves to Liberia, a plan advocated by many abolitionists, struck her as absurd: Their only hope for the future lay on the road to Christianity, and in Africa they would revert to heathenism. Though Mrs. Stowe's opposition to slavery had hardened, she still clung to the opinion that gradual emancipation achieved through religion and education provided the only genuine solution. The economy of the South would be disrupted when the slaves departed, and gradual emanicipation was the only fair way to protect plantation owners, who would need time to find other sources of labor.

Apparently unable to assess the intensity of feeling in both North and South, Mrs. Stowe believed that in writing her book she was performing a healing function. Extremists might hate her, but *Uncle Tom's Cabin* would surely appeal to moderates in both sections of the country; when they banded together, slavery could be destroyed in the manner least harmful to everyone concerned.

—Noel B. Gerson, *Harriet Beecher Stowe: A Biography* (New York: Praeger, 1976), pp. 68–69

ELIZABETH AMMONS ON STOWE'S EXTOLLING OF MOTHERHOOD

[Elizabeth Ammons is a professor of English at Tufts University and the author of *Edith Wharton's Argument with America* (1980) and *Conflicting Stories: American Women Writers at the Turn into the Twentieth Century* (1991). In this extract, Ammons studies Stowe's belief that she was chosen to write *Uncle Tom's Cabin* because she was a woman and a mother.]

Late in the nineteenth century Harriet Beecher Stowe announced that God wrote *Uncle Tom's Cabin* (1852). The novel by then seemed too monumental even to its author to have been imagined by one woman. Earlier in her life, in contrast, Stowe had no doubt that she wrote the subversive book or that she was inspired to write it, despite marital and household irritations, precisely because she was a woman.

In a letter to her husband ten years before the publication of the novel, and almost ninety years before Virginia Woolf's famous declaration of independence on behalf of all women writers in *A Room of One's Own* (1929), Harriet Beecher Stowe said: "There is one thing I must suggest. If I am to write, I must have a room to myself, which shall be *my* room." With her room came the mission to write what became America's best-known novel, and the mission fell to her, she believed, because she was a mother. She recalled for one of her grown children, "I well remember the winter you were a baby and I was writing 'Uncle Tom's Cabin.' My heart was bursting with the anguish excited by the cruelty and injustice our nation was showing to the slave, and praying God to let me do a little and to cause my cry for them to be heard. I remember many a night weeping over you as you lay sleeping beside me, and I thought of the slave mothers whose babies were torn from them." One of her seven children died while still an infant. She says: "It was at his dying bed and at his grave that I learned what a poor slave mother may feel when her child is torn away from her." Authors' remarks on the genesis of their work sometimes prove misleading, but not in this case. Stowe's insistence on maternal experience as the generative principle of *Uncle Tom's Cabin* identifies the ethical center of the novel, and helps explain the unusual, and often misunderstood, characterization of Tom.

Stowe's protagonist is gentle, pious, chaste, domestic, long-suffering and self-sacrificing. In a nineteenth-century heroine, those attributes would not seem strange. Associate them, however, with the hero of an American novel, a genre sifted for its Adamic rebels, and readers' complacence can evaporate. Indeed, the farther *Uncle Tom's Cabin* has moved in time from the historical reality of chattel slavery, the more obvious and the more criticized "effeminate" Tom has become; and whether it is stated in so many words or not, often what is objected to is the fact that Stowe makes him a heroine instead of a hero. ⟨. . .⟩

Stowe's treatment of maternal values may at a glance look unremarkable. Nearly every page of *Uncle Tom's Cabin* hymns the virtues of Mother, the revered figure whose benign influence over domestic life in the nineteenth century was conveniently supposed, and promoted, to redress the abuses against humanity engendered in the masculine, money-making realm. Stowe, however, refuses to appoint Mother the handmaiden of Mammon in *Uncle Tom's Cabin*. Instead, she enlists the cult of motherhood in the unorthodox cause of challenging, not accommodating, the patriarchal status quo. Like her sister Catharine Beecher, Harriet Beecher Stowe displays in *Uncle Tom's Cabin* a facility for converting essentially repressive concepts of femininity into a positive (and activist) alternative sys-

tem of values in which woman figures not merely as the moral superior of man, his inspirer, but as the model for him in the new millennium about to dawn.
—Elizabeth Ammons, "Heroines in *Uncle Tom's Cabin*," *American Literature* 49, No. 2 (May 1977): 161–63

ANN DOUGLAS ON STOWE AS FEMINIST

[Ann Douglas (b. 1942), a professor of English at Columbia University, has written *The Feminization of American Culture* (1977) and *Terrible Honesty: Mongrel Manhattan in the 1920s* (1995). In this extract, Douglas maintains that Stowe represented a powerful voice not only for the abolition of slavery but for the advancement of women.]

The multifaceted question of *Uncle Tom's* greatness is not a trivial or irresolvable one. To put it simply, *everything* involved in the writing and in the subject matter of *Uncle Tom's Cabin* was controversial: Stowe's sex, or more specifically, the proper limits of style and material that members of her sex should observe as authors; slavery and racism as religious and political issues; and the form proper to the American novel in contrast with its English counterpart.

Stowe was the most prominent member of what was only the second generation of American women novelists, and the first of their number to attain literary distinction. By 1815 England had already produced Maria Edgeworth, Fanny Burney, and Jane Austen; well flanked by a host of talented minor feminine writers, they established the fact that English women could write novels and even help determine the novel's scope and form. No American women authors of the period can justly be placed in their company. In the late 1930s and 1940s, the English critic F. R. Leavis began his influential discussion of the "great tradition" of the English novel, starting with Austen. In 1923 D. H. Lawrence, brilliantly establishing the legitimacy of "Classic American Literature" in his study of the same name, took James Fenimore Cooper as his first novelist (Cooper started to publish in 1820); Lawrence did not include a single woman writer in the course of a survey that ended with Whitman. While the second generation of Lawrence's chosen (male) authors of American classics—Poe, Hawthorne, Melville, Dana, and Whitman—were writing in the 1840s, 1850s, and 1860s, Dickens and Thackeray were at work in England. But so were the Brontës and George Eliot; indeed, George Eliot is the pivotal figure in Leavis's attempt to define the English novel in its major phase in *The Great Tradition*.

Whether or not Leavis or Lawrence were altogether right in their choices or their analyses, one fact is clear: by 1850, when Harriet Beecher Stowe began *Uncle Tom,* English women were writing profitably and well; American women were writing, at best, profitably. For many reasons they were more rigidly confined by conventional stereotypes of femininity than were their English counterparts. Where English women writers took male noms de plume, such as Currer Bell and George Eliot, American authoresses adopted pretty, alliterative, ultrafeminine floral aliases plainly intended to disarm criticism and disavow ambition. "Fanny Fern" and "Grace Greenwood" could not insist to their readers, as Charlotte Brontë did, that they came before their audience "as author[s] only." Never lacking in energy, the American women by and large stuck to the themes of piety, deference, and domesticity prescribed for their sex. Harriet Beecher Stowe, however, was a correspondent of George Eliot's and a friend of Elizabeth Barrett Browning's, and she deserved to be. She always wrote under her own name and took up whatever subject matter compelled her. Lawbreaking was one of the major themes of her first two novels, *Uncle Tom's Cabin* and *Dred,* and she shared this fascination not with her feminine literary peers but with Hawthorne and Melville.

Stowe was not a declared feminist, although the link between antislavery and the women's movement was a vital one. Women's antislavery groups were formed as auxiliaries to the men's antislavery organizations in the early and mid-1830s. As their members grew more conscious of the discrimination that their male cohorts exercised against them, these all-female groups became the seedbed of the feminist crusade of the late 1840s and 1850s. Stowe—eccentric, moody, dreamy, and energetic by turns—was a maverick; she shied away from all associations and all labels. Yet *Uncle Tom's Cabin,* in its inception, style, and substance, is a powerfully feminist book.

> —Ann Douglas, "Introduction: The Art of Controversy," *Uncle Tom's Cabin* (New York: Penguin, 1981), pp. 11–13

THOMAS F. GOSSETT ON THE RECEPTION OF *UNCLE TOM'S CABIN*

[Thomas F. Gossett (b. 1916) is a former professor of English at Trinity University in San Antonio, Texas, and the author of a landmark work on racism, *Race: The History of an Idea in America* (1963). In this extract from his exhaustive study of the reception of *Uncle Tom's Cabin,* Gossett concludes that the reactions to Stowe's novels over the years are an index of the prevalence of racism in this country.]

To read the opinions of *Uncle Tom's Cabin* which have been expressed over the past 130 years is something like examining a history of racism in America for this period, at least racism as it has been applied to blacks. J. C. Furnas was right when he said that *Uncle Tom's Cabin* was like a three-stage rocket—it was first powerful as a novel, then as a play, and eventually in the twentieth century as a film. It is doubtful that any work of American literature has received such a variety of interpretations, both in the reviews and criticisms it has generated and in the many ways in which it has been adapted as a play. When the novel was published in 1852, even northern reviewers in surprisingly large numbers criticized it for what they felt were exaggerated accounts of the evils of slavery. Nevertheless, it is obvious that Stowe's book was a powerful force in changing the minds of white northerners and in alerting opinion abroad to the evils of American slavery.

For a long time the almost universal detestation of *Uncle Tom's Cabin* prevented all but a few readers in the South from examining it from any point of view except that of its alleged unfairness to the South and to slavery. When the Civil War was over and the white South had time to calm down, readers and critics there discovered that the novel contained ideas about blacks which might be used to suggest a more sympathetic interpretation of their own view of history. With a little judicious manipulation, many of these white southern interpreters convinced themselves that they could find in *Uncle Tom's Cabin* itself sufficient evidence to justify their own conviction that blacks ought not to have a status in society equal to that of whites. They did not wish to return to slavery, but neither did they wish to give the blacks full rights as citizens. The white South eventually came to admit, at least by implication, that slavery had been wrong, disunion had been wrong, and therefore the South's decision to initiate the Civil War had been wrong. On the other hand, they reasoned, it did not follow that the antebellum white South had been wrong in its belief in the inherent inferiority of blacks.

In the late nineteenth and early twentieth centuries, a substantial number of white northern critics of *Uncle Tom's Cabin* had also changed their opinions and had moved closer to those held by white southerners. A view frequently expressed, especially after northern disillusion with the Reconstruction of the South, was that slavery had been an evil institution and Stowe had been right to indict it. On the other hand, a surprisingly large number of white northern critics came to think Stowe had been wrong in making the black characters in her novel too noble, amiable, and intelligent to be credible. If these critics had said that her black characters generally had better qualities than people of any race, they might have had a point. Usually, however, they merely said that her black characters were presented as being better than real blacks.

In the last forty years, the current of opinion toward Stowe and *Uncle Tom's Cabin* falls chiefly into three categories. Black critics and scholars strongly reject the novel, deploring the frequent recourse to racist explanations of the traits of the characters, especially those of the blacks. A great many white critics—probably a majority—also reject the novel but principally because they find it almost wholly lacking in literary merit. There is a third group, however, who have something like the enthusiasm of earlier critics for both the author and her book. Nearly all of these critics are white, and to those who reject the novel on literary grounds, these critics say that Stowe's faults are a matter of style rather than of substance. They argue that while she used the form of the sentimental and domestic novel, she was able to transcend that form because she had a broad grasp of human nature and was able to analyze both institutions and individual characters with great insight. To the black critics who deplore the novel, the white critics who admire it generally concede that it contains serious faults in its interpretation of the black characters. They argue, however, that Stowe's racism belongs to her time and place. They see her as struggling, and with considerable success, to free herself from it. Properly understood, they argue, the racism is not sufficient to invalidate the novel, and they conclude that Stowe was able not merely to analyze slavery perceptively but to present credible characters, black and white, reacting to a monstrous institution.

—Thomas F. Gossett, Uncle Tom's Cabin *and American Culture* (Dallas: Southern Methodist University Press, 1985), pp. 409–11

JOHN R. ADAMS ON *UNCLE TOM'S CABIN* AS A VICTORIAN NOVEL

[John R. Adams (b. 1900) is the author of critical studies of Edward Everett Hale (1977) and Harriet Beecher Stowe (1963); the following extract is taken from a revised (1989) edition of the latter work. Here, Adams believes that *Uncle Tom's Cabin* was, to its original readers, not a political tract but a story in the sentimental Victorian tradition.]

Only a child can read *Uncle Tom's Cabin* without preconceptions. William Dean Howells, aged fourteen, read it under ideal conditions, week by week, as a serial story by an unknown author. Each chapter was fresh, the picture was clear, the reader could not know what would come next or how the story would end. Above all, the original *Uncle Tom's Cabin* serial was a story, not a controversy. It induced its readers—a special interest group—to weep a lot, laugh a little, become indignant, and perhaps even resolve to lead a better life. As a brand new book, however, offered to the nation and the world, it reached a hostile as well as a sympathetic audience, becoming at once a document with political implications. Over the years it has been the most discussed book in American history, and by now no person who reads it or, certainly, writes about it can see it with the fresh approach of Howells and other enthusiastic readers of the *National Era*. Every synopsis is an analysis, every chapter a question.

What is *Uncle Tom's Cabin* about? To the original readers it was about slavery in the South, a story about weak and wicked people, strong and virtuous people, from fiends to saints. It pleaded for the end of slavery, with the narrator often speaking to the reader, making herself a character in the story. With emancipation accomplished and the original purpose attained (though not in the way Stowe had intended or foreseen) new readers have discovered other themes of enduring importance: family life, racial differences, the superiority of women, personal and social redemption. The meaning of *Uncle Tom's Cabin* has become as debated as its factual accuracy was contested when Stowe wrote it as a description of the life of its time.

Yet the book is a story, no matter how many messages it carries, and the substance could be compressed into a paragraph for some technical purposes, the design is so easily stated. It is one of the Victorian novels in which, according to a common practice, the adventures of two groups of characters are alternated to give an inclusive picture of society and to provide a variety of emotional appeal.
—John R. Adams, *Harriet Beecher Stowe* (Boston: Twayne, 1963; rev. 1989), pp. 24–25

[Josephine Donovan (b. 1941), a professor of English at the University of Maine, is the author of *Feminine Literary Criticism: Explorations in Theory* (1975), *Feminist Theory: The Intellectual Traditions of American Feminism* (1985), and a study of *Uncle Tom's Cabin* (1991), from which the following extract is taken. Here, Donovan examines the theme of evil in the novel and the different characters' responses to it.]

Masterpiece literature also often provides a rich variety and depth of characterization; it often presents a dense, detailed, and convincing sense of reality—whether psychological reality, an epic sense of setting, or the complexities of moral life; and finally, it must have an underlying architectonic integrity—that is, it must exhibit throughout an inherent design, or what Aristotle called *dianoia* or thought.

Uncle Tom's Cabin satisfies these criteria. First, it engages in serious, universal themes. The central issue in the novel is slavery, but Stowe clearly views slavery as a specific manifestation of the problem of evil. Therefore, while the institution of slavery has been abolished, the novel retains its relevance today because the broader issue of the existence of political evil and suffering remains. Indeed, ⟨. . .⟩ it is because of its unflinching examination of this issue that the novel bears a haunting contemporaneity for the twentieth-century reader. It still works to enlarge our moral understanding.

Through her characters Stowe presents a series of possible responses to the moral issue of the existence of evil. George Harris, for example, a slave who escapes north, takes an essentially atheistic approach, saying that a benevolent God would not permit such atrocities as slavery to exist; Uncle Tom takes a Christian approach, that suffering is redemptive and that evil will be atoned for; the slave woman Cassy believes that violence is the only means by which evil can be vanquished; Mrs. Shelby, the Kentucky plantation mistress, and a number of Quakers who operate on the underground railway advocate nonviolent resistance and personal acts to alleviate suffering; St. Clare, a relatively benign plantation owner, counsels an apathetic stance, saying there is nothing one can do to end suffering and oppression. In short, Stowe develops a range of responses to the issue of evil, and her development of them, as we shall see, is done at a level of great moral sophistication.

Second, even a superficial reading of the novel reveals the richness and variety of Stowe's characterization. This is indeed one of her great strengths as a writer. Over a hundred characters are fully developed—from every class and from several regions, including free and slave blacks, northern and southern whites. Similarly, the epic scope of the novel, the range of its settings, and the prodigious detail of its realism provide the reader with an unrivaled sense of the texture of nineteenth-century American life.

Finally, Stowe's novel is carefully constructed according to an identifiable moral architecture. Few critics have recognized the powerful organizing design that undergirds the work. Stowe conceived *Uncle Tom's Cabin* as an *argument* against slavery; it is constructed according to a rhetorical pattern of moral antithesis. It proceeds by means of a series of antithetical characters or sets of characters, building dialectically to the climactic, allegorical final scenes in which Uncle Tom, who has assumed the status of a Christ figure, contends with Simon Legree, the Antichrist. The powerful confrontation between the two, in which Tom endures physical death but gains a spiritual triumph ("the sharp thorns became rays of glory"), brings Stowe's work to an effective moral and formal resolution.

We read *Uncle Tom's Cabin* today through an overlay of twentieth-century atrocities—the Nazi concentration camps, the Soviet gulags, Hiroshima, My Lai. In an era when torture of resisting political prisoners is not uncommon, Uncle Tom's refusal to capitulate to Legree's torture as well as his refusal to engage in violence take on new meaning.

—Josephine Donovan, Uncle Tom's Cabin: *Evil, Affliction and Redemptive Love* (Boston: Twayne, 1991), pp. 12–13

[Jennifer L. Jenkins, at the time she wrote the following article, was a Ph.D. candidate at the University of Arizona. Here, Jenkins asserts that, although Stowe proclaims the ideal of motherhood in *Uncle Tom's Cabin,* the actual mothers in the novel dominate their families by fear, not love.]

Stowe insists in *Uncle Tom's Cabin* that the divisive culture and politics of mid-nineteenth-century America are merely symptoms of a troubled family. Preoccupied with home and family in her own life, she proposes these two forces as common elements in both black and white life in her fictional antebellum South. In *American Woman's Home* (1869) she would promote a domestic separation of labor, in which men build houses and women oversee the households: "The family state then, is the aptest earthly illustration of the heavenly kingdom, and in it woman is its chief minister. . . . To man is appointed the out-door labor." Woman, the "chief minister," rules this domestic heaven, while man is expelled from the maternal "kingdom" to the world of work. Male guilt for abandoning religion and family in favor of trade, according to Barbara Welter, produced this ministerial ideal of the feminine: "He could salve his conscience," she argues, "by reflecting that he had left behind a hostage, not only to fortune, but to all the values which he held so dear and treated so lightly. Woman, in the cult of True Womanhood presented by the women's magazines, gift annuals and religious literature of the nineteenth century, was the hostage in the home." This "cult of True Womanhood" or "cult of domesticity" idealized a pious indoor life of refinement and efficiency designed to please the master, and to transform the mistress into an "angel in the house."

Like any cult, however, domesticity had its dangers. Though the house could symbolize inherited identity for a man, for a woman it often threatened identity itself. With the rise of manufacturing and city-based industry, women, who had once shared pioneer life out-of-doors with men, increasingly were sent to their rooms. For women writers, in particular, the house became an utterly other sort of icon. Built by father, brother or husband, the house could soon prove prison, madhouse, seraglio, or charnel house to its female inhabitants. By the nineteenth century, the enclosure of frontier forests had given way to equally oppressive walls and roofs. Small wonder, then, that houses could become places of some distaste and horror in the female imagination. In *Uncle Tom's Cabin* domestic confinement produces uncanny tendencies both in houses and in the women who run them. So, while Stowe subscribes to contemporary sentimental ideologies of domesticity, her novel actually posits domestic space as a gothic site.

As in most domestic novels, mothers are the agents of power in *Uncle Tom's Cabin*. Stowe contends polemically that motherly love is sacred, demonstrated in pity, tenderness, and prayers—an argument consistent with her image of a domestic heaven. Appropriating this trope, Jane Tompkins has argued that *Uncle Tom's Cabin* offers to "reorganize culture from a woman's point of view," and thus becomes a feminine hagiography of sorts: "It is the *summa theologica* of nineteenth-century America's religion of domesticity, a brilliant redaction of the culture's favorite story about itself—the story of salvation through motherly love. Out of the ideological materials at their disposal, the sentimental novelists elaborated a myth that gave women the central position of power and authority in the culture." This good, Christian mother is the maternal type that Tompkins has found to be a compelling icon in American culture. Indeed, Stowe herself attributed such motherliness to women of all classes and races.

Yet the mothers of *Uncle Tom's Cabin* appropriate this position of authority not by means of love, but of fear. As Julia Kristeva notes, the Christianized notion of maternal love offers "the whole range of love-types from sublimation to asceticism and masochism." One loving, harmless mother does appear in the novel: the Quaker Rachel Halliday. She stands as the cultural ideal of motherhood against which all other mothers in the novel may be measured. When Stowe's women deviate from this benign stereotype they become gothic images of the feminine, and degenerate into extremes: either the madwoman-vampire, or the self-sacrificing mamma who obsessively loves her children to death. The good mothers become particularly horrible, due to the suffocating intensity of their maternal love.

The effect of this ambivalent maternal force is sameness: the vampire and the angel become indistinguishable. From Mrs. Shelby to Mrs. Legree, Stowe's mothers neglect, deceive, or abuse their offspring. As the plot of the novel moves the characters from one mother to the next, an encyclopedia of domestic collapse takes shape. Angelic but insidious mammas meet the underground railroad, while the river journeys on the Mississippi and the Red carry Tom from termagant to shrew to madwoman. Such domestic disruption and collapse fractures the plot and subverts the narrative of *Uncle Tom's Cabin.*

—Jennifer L. Jenkins, "Failed Mothers and Fallen Houses: The Crisis of Domesticity in *Uncle Tom's Cabin," ESQ* 38, No. 2 (Second Quarter 1992): 162–64

GLADYS SHERMAN LEWIS ON PURITAN GENRES AND THE STRUCTURE OF *UNCLE TOM'S CABIN*

[Gladys Sherman Lewis is a professor of English at the University of Central Oklahoma and the author of *Message, Messenger, and Response* (1994), a study of *Uncle Tom's Cabin* from which the following extract is taken. Here, Lewis argues that the novel is based upon several literary genres from the Puritan age, including the sermon and the propaganda tract.]

Puritan genres provide a selection of forms which have accepted conventions in their literary treatment. By manipulating and rearranging several Puritan conventions, Harriet Beecher Stowe transformed in *Uncle Tom's Cabin* the ways in which antebellum America perceived slavery and viewed that culture. Her strategies allow her to articulate social protest, illustrate a social problem, illuminate both the inner and outer context of characters affected by both the protest and the problem of slavery, propose individual and group resolutions, and issue a national call for social change based on these results. Sermon as genre carries the social protest; the captivity narrative defines the social problem; the spiritual autobiography, confessions, and conversion narratives furnish the effect of slavery on the characters and serve to illustrate their resolutions; and jeremiad rhetoric charges the nation to make a response to the issue which influences every individual. By providing the form and proposing the content for the protest against slavery in American culture, the Puritan genres in *Uncle Tom's Cabin* shape both a master design and a master plot which Stowe proposes to the audience as ways to join in a collaboration against the mutual social problem. The design comes from her Christian vision for the world; the plot develops from the stories of people in that world. Although *Uncle Tom's Cabin* draws upon Puritan literary conventions, its content does not, but that practice is conventional in itself because it fits the Puritan pattern of using cultural, human material to deal with the spiritual.

Her novel's master design has three basic parts which are always assumed from any of the sermonic characteristics and must be understood as a divine triad which structures the master plot of the characters. Time is forward moving and based in history which is shaped by Christian millenial eschatology; heaven is the home of the soul and the ideal place; and trinitarian interdependence and mutuality in the Godhead provide a model for ideal human relationships. The complex biblical base which permeates the book with specific citations, allusions, and illustrations in the depiction of characters and in characters's descriptions of themselves and each other consistently point to this three-part scheme which serves to reflect the novel.

In the first part of the paradigm, Stowe holds to a Genesis-creation with time proceeding on a line to its end: "He shall not fail nor be discouraged / Till He have set judgment in the earth" (Isaiah 42:4). After the biblical fall from grace, Christ, the redeeming sacrifice sent by God, the Father, descends into the world to return in ascension, assuring the security of time in historical reality which proceeds in a linear direction to an apocalyptic judgment and beyond for eternity: "I am the resurrection and the Life; he that believeth in me, though he were dead, yet shall he live" (John 11:25).

The second part of her design emphasizes that the soul has a place of destination during its travels through life: heaven as ultimate home. No matter what happens in experience, the hope for heaven as perfect home and rest remains constantly before the soul: "Let not your heart be troubled. In my Father's house are many mansions. I go to prepare a place for you" (John 14:21–22).

The last segment concerns the interaction of mutually distinct spheres in power, love, and activity among the Trinity that forms her ideal for relationships which grant feeling and ethical behavior: "Father, forgive them, for they know not what they do" (Luke 23:34). With a circular movement that travels in both directions, God, the Father, giver of law, order, system, and Old Testament revelation, communicates with God, the Son, Jesus Christ, who personifies grace, love, redemption, and New Testament ethics, and relates to God, the Holy Spirit, the paraclete, enabling believers to enact the New Testament liberty from the law through loving obedience to the ethical demands of faith.

The Christian Trinitarian model for relationships proscribes the love and morality encountered by characters as they move through time and pause in different geographical settings where, while exposed to feelings, they learn morality. Stowe's mental habits reflect Puritan Ramist logic. She constantly balances expressions of opposites: power/submission, bond/free, public/private, aggression/tenderness, dominance/nurture. In human relational paradigms, she arranges people in families as units both of individuals and groups which enact mutually affirming dichotomies of power/weakness, male/female, bond/free, and public/private.

In *Uncle Tom's Cabin* the sermon and the propaganda tract act in tandem with the conflict produced from accounts of captivity narratives, spiritual autobiographies, confessions, and conversion narratives. Sermon structures carry both the law, as its characteristics appear in its various parts through the book, and the protest, as a jeremiad against slavery in its entirety; captivity narratives present the problem; spiritual autobiographies and confessions describe the process of confronting slavery in its many shapes; conversion provides resolutions of the conflicts to propose that one feel right, act right, and do right; and the propaganda tract reinforces the legitimacy of the resolution as a viable solution for the protest presented by the problem and its processes. As a jeremiad, the sermon diagnoses the illness as slavery; the Puritan narratives show how to treat it; and the sermon as propaganda tract presents the prognosis as Stowe argues for the adaptations and adjustments which she considers to be viable solutions. The sermon controls the form of the novel by its use of the Bible through citation and allusion, character typologies, and structure and style of the text. As lay sermons, the captivity narratives restate the master design's ideology in light of individual experience. Spiritual autobiographies and confessions, as stories of conflict with perverted law which has supplanted ideal rule, propose the culture's master plot, that of a nation of people who are exemplary because they internalize the governance and behavior of the master design. Individual conversion narratives implement the sermon's master design and validate the master plot of a nation converted to justice and morality to be God's light to the world in a new covenant where love and feeling in moral codes are more important than doctrine.

—Gladys Sherman Lewis, *Message, Messenger, and Response: Puritan Forms and Cultural Reformation in Harriet Beecher Stowe's* Uncle Tom's Cabin (Lanham, MD: University Press of America, 1994), pp. 13–16

Books by
Harriet Beecher Stowe

Primary Geography for Children (with Catherine Beecher).
1833.

A New England Sketch. 1834.

*The Mayflower; or, Sketches of Scenes and Characters among
the Descendants of the Pilgrims.* 1843.

Uncle Tom's Cabin; or, Life among the Lowly. 1852. 2 vols.

Earthly Care, a Heavenly Discipline. 1852.

The Two Altars; or, Two Pictures in One. 1852.

History of the Edmondson Family. c. 1852.

A Key to Uncle Tom's Cabin: *Presenting the Original Facts and
Documents upon Which the Story Is Founded.* 1853, 1854.

*Uncle Sam's Emancipation; Earthly Care, a Heavenly Discipline;
and Other Sketches.* 1853.

The Coral King. 1853.

Letter to the Ladies' New Anti-Slavery Society of Glasgow.
c. 1853.

Sunny Memories of Foreign Lands. 1854. 2 vols.

Notice of the Boston Anti-Slavery Bazaar. c. 1854.

First Geography for Children. 1855.

The May Flower and Miscellaneous Writings. 1855.

The Christian Slave. 1855.

What Should We Do without the Bible? c. 1855.

Dred: A Tale of the Great Dismal Swamp. 1856. 2 vols.

Mrs. H. B. Stowe on Dr. Monod and the American Tract Society; Considered in Relation to American Slavery. 1858.

My Expectation. 1858.

My Strength. 1858.

Things That Cannot Be Shaken. 1858.

Strong Consolation; or, God a Refuge and Strength. 1858.

A Word to the Sorrowful. 1858.

Our Charley, and What to Do with Him. 1858.

Harriet Beecher Stowe on the American Board of Commissioners for Foreign Missions. c. 1858.

The Minister's Wooing. 1859.

The Pearl of Orr's Island: A Story of the Coast of Maine. 1862.

Agnes of Sorrento. 1862.

A Reply to The Affectionate and Christian Address of Many Thousands of Women of Great Britain and Ireland, to Their Sisters, the Women of the United States: *In Behalf of Many Thousands of American Women.* 1863.

Primitive Christian Experience. c. 1863.

The Ravages of a Carpet. c. 1864.

House and Home Papers. 1865.

Stories about Our Dogs. 1865.

Little Foxes. 1866.

Religious Poems. 1867.

The Daisy's First Winter and Other Stories. 1867.

Queer Little People. 1867.

The Chimney-Corner. 1868.

Men of Our Times; or, Leading Patriots of the Day. 1868.

Oldtown Folks. 1869.

The American Woman's Home; or, Principles of Domestic Science (with Catherine E. Beecher). 1869, 1870 (as *Principles of Domestic Science*), 1874 (as *The New Housekeeper's Manual*).

Lady Byron Vindicated: A History of the Byron Controversy from Its Beginning in 1816 to the Present Time. 1870.

Little Pussy Willow. 1870.

Pink and White Tyranny: A Society Novel. 1871.

My Wife and I; or, Harry Henderson's History. 1871.

Have You Seen It? Letter from Mrs. Stowe to Miss Kate Reignolds. c. 1871.

Sam Lawson's Oldtown Fireside Stories. 1872.

"He's Coming To-morrow." c. 1872.

Palmetto-Leaves. 1873.

Woman in Sacred History. 1873.

We and Our Neighbors; or, The Records of an Unfashionable Street. 1875.

Betty Bright Idea. 1876.

Footsteps of the Master. 1877.

Poganuc People: Their Loves and Lives. 1878.

A Dog's Mission; or, The Story of the Old Avery House, and Other Stories. 1881.

Flowers and Fruit from the Writings of Harriet Beecher Stowe. Ed. Abbie H. Fairfield. 1888.

Dialogues and Scenes from the Writings of Harriet Beecher Stowe. Ed. Emily Weaver. 1889.

Life of Harriet Beecher Stowe Compiled from Her Letters and Journals. Ed. Charles Edward Stowe. 1889.

Writings. 1896. 16 vols.

Life and Letters. Ed. Annie Fields. 1897.

Collected Poems. Ed. John Michael Moran, Jr. 1967.

Regional Sketches: New England and Florida. Ed. John R. Adams. 1972.

Uncle Tom's Cabin; The Minister's Wooing; Oldtown Folks. 1982.

Works about Harriet Beecher Stowe and Uncle Tom's Cabin

Anderson, Beatrice A. "Uncle Tom: A Hero at Last." *American Transcendental Quarterly* 5 (1991): 95–108.

Askeland, Lori. "Remodeling the Model Home in *Uncle Tom's Cabin* and *Beloved*." *American Literature* 64 (1992): 785–805.

Baldwin, James. "Everybody's Protest Novel." *Partisan Review* 16 (1949): 578–85.

Banks, Marva. "*Uncle Tom's Cabin* and Antebellum Black Response." In *Readers in History: Nineteenth-Century American Literature and the Contexts of Response*, ed. James L. Machor. Baltimore: Johns Hopkins University Press, 1993, pp. 209–27.

Bellin, Joshua D. "Up to Heaven's Gate, Down in Earth's Dust: The Politics of Judgment in *Uncle Tom's Cabin*." *American Literature* 65 (1993): 275–95.

Brown, Gillian. "Getting in the Kitchen with Dinah: Domestic Politics in *Uncle Tom's Cabin*." *American Quarterly* 36 (1984): 503–23.

Camfield, Gregg. "The Moral Aesthetics of Sentimentality: A Missing Key to *Uncle Tom's Cabin*." *Nineteenth-Century Literature* 43 (1988–89): 319–45.

DeCanio, Stephen J. "*Uncle Tom's Cabin*: A Reappraisal." *Centennial Review* 34 (1990): 587–93.

Fiedler, Leslie. "Home as Heaven, Home as Hell: Uncle Tom's Canon." In *Rewriting the Dream: Reflections on the Changing American Canon*, ed. W. M. Verhoeven. Amsterdam: Rodopi, 1992, pp. 22–42.

Fluck, Winfried. "The Power and Failure of Representation in Harriet Beecher Stowe's *Uncle Tom's Cabin*." *New Literary History* 23 (1992): 319–38.

Grinstein, Alexander. "*Uncle Tom's Cabin* and Harriet Beecher Stowe: Beating Fantasies and Thoughts of Death." *American Imago* 40 (1983): 115–44.

Hedrick, Joan B. *Harriet Beecher Stowe: A Life.* New York: Oxford University Press, 1994.

Hirsch, Stephen A. "Uncle Tomitudes: The Popular Reaction to *Uncle Tom's Cabin.*" *Studies in the American Renaissance,* 1978, pp. 303–30.

Hovet, Theodore R. "Modernization and the American Fall into Slavery in *Uncle Tom's Cabin.*" *New England Quarterly* 54 (1981): 499–518.

Jehlen, Myra. "The Family Militant: Domesticity versus Slavery in *Uncle Tom's Cabin.*" *Criticism* 31 (1989): 383–400.

Joswick, Thomas P. " 'The Crown without the Conflict': Religious Values and Moral Reasoning in *Uncle Tom's Cabin.*" *Nineteenth-Century Literature* 39 (1984–85): 253–74.

Kimball, Gayle. *The Religious Ideas of Harriet Beecher Stowe: Her Gospel of Womanhood.* New York: Mellen Press, 1982.

Kirkham, E. Bruce. *The Building of* Uncle Tom's Cabin. Knoxville: University of Tennessee Press, 1977.

Krog, Carl E. "Women, Slaves, and Family in *Uncle Tom's Cabin:* Symbolic Battleground in Antebellum America." *Midwest Quarterly* 31 (1990): 252–69.

Lant, Kathleen Margaret. "The Unsung Hero of *Uncle Tom's Cabin.*" *American Studies* 28 (1987): 47–71.

Lowance, Mason I., Jr.; Wesbrook, Ellen E.; and De Prospo, R. C., ed. *The Stowe Debate: Rhetorical Strategies in* Uncle Tom's Cabin. Amherst: University of Massachusetts Press, 1994.

McConnell, Frank D. "Uncle Tom and the Avant-Garde." *Massachusetts Review* 16 (1975): 732–45.

Moers, Ellen. *Harriet Beecher Stowe and American Literature.* Hartford, CT: Stowe-Day Foundation, 1978.

Prior, Moody E. "Mrs. Stowe's Uncle Tom." *Critical Inquiry* 5 (1978–79): 635–50.

Railton, Stephen. "Mothers, Husbands, and Uncle Tom." *Georgia Review* 38 (1984): 129–44.

Reynolds, Moira Davison. Uncle Tom's Cabin *and Mid-Nineteenth Century United States: Pen and Conscience.* Jefferson, NC: McFarland, 1985.

Romero, Lora. "Bio-Political Resistance in Domestic Ideology and *Uncle Tom's Cabin.*" *American Literary History* 1 (1989): 715–34.

Sarson, Steven. "Harriet Beecher Stowe and American Slavery." *New Comparison* 7 (Summer 1989): 33–45.

Short, Bryan C. "Stowe, Dickinson, and the Rhetoric of Modernism." *Arizona Quarterly* 47 (1991): 1–16.

Smylie, James H. "*Uncle Tom's Cabin* Revisited: The Bible, the Romantic Imagination, and the Sympathies of Christ." *Interpretation* 27 (1973): 67–85.

Sundquist, Eric J., ed. *New Essays on* Uncle Tom's Cabin. Cambridge: Cambridge University Press, 1986.

Wagenknecht, Edward. *Harriet Beecher Stowe: The Known and the Unknown.* New York: Oxford University Press, 1965.

Wardley, Lynn. "Relic, Fetish, Femmage: The Aesthetics of Sentiment in the Work of Stowe." *Yale Journal of Criticism* 5 (1992): 165–91.

Warhol, Robyn R. "Politics and Persuasion: *Uncle Tom's Cabin* as a Realist Novel." *Essays in Literature* 13 (1986): 283–98.

White, Isabelle. "The Uses of Death in *Uncle Tom's Cabin.*" *American Studies* 26 (1985): 5–17.

Whitney, Lisa. "In the Shadow of *Uncle Tom's Cabin:* Stowe's Vision of Slavery from the Great Dismal Swamp." *New England Quarterly* 66 (1993): 552–69.

Yellin, Jean Fagan. "Harriet Beecher Stowe." In Yellin's *The Intricate Knot: Black Figures in American Literature.* New York: New York University Press, 1972, pp. 121–53.

Zwarg, Christina. "Fathering the Blackface in *Uncle Tom's Cabin.*" *Novel* 22 (1989): 274–87.

Index of
Themes and Ideas

LEGREE, SIMON: as Antichrist, 56; Augustine St. Clare contrasted with, 34–35; haunted garret of, 20–21; mother of, 20; and his role in the novel, 5–6, 18–21, 36; Tom sold to, 18, 24

LIBERIA, and its role in the novel, 21–22, 45

LITTLE WOMEN (Alcott), and how it compares, 38

LOKER, TOM, and his role in the novel, 12, 15, 34

MAMMY, and her role in the novel, 15

MARKS, and his role in the novel, 12, 15, 34, 40

MOTHERHOOD, as theme, 12, 16, 21, 47–49, 57–59

PIONEERS, THE (Cooper), and how it compares, 40

PRUE, and her role in the novel, 16

ST. CLARE, ALFRED, and his role in the novel, 16–17, 41

ST. CLARE, AUGUSTINE: death of, 18; and Eva's death, 17–18; and evil, 56; Legree contrasted with, 34–35; and his role in the novel, 15–18, 20, 23

ST. CLARE, EVANGELINE ("Little Eva"): death of, 17, 23, 37; and her role in the novel, 14–18, 23, 44; Tom's relationship with, 16–18, 19, 20; and Topsy, 16–18, 24

ST. CLARE, HENRIQUE, and his role in the novel, 16–17, 41

ST. CLARE, MARIE, and her role in the novel, 15–18, 24, 41

ST. CLARE, OPHELIA, and her role in the novel, 15–18, 21, 24, 41

SCARLET LETTER, THE (Hawthorne), and how it compares, 6

SHELBY, GEORGE, and his role in the novel, 11, 13, 21

SHELBY, MR., and his role in the novel, 10–13, 16, 18, 21, 42, 45

SHELBY, MRS., and her role in the novel, 10–13, 16, 18, 21, 42, 45, 55, 59

STOWE, HARRIET BEECHER: as feminist, 49–51, 53; life of, 7–9; as mother, 47–48; slavery experienced by, 7–8, 26–28

SUSAN, and her role in the novel, 18–21

TOPSY, and her role in the novel, 16–18, 24, 35

TWAIN, MARK, Stowe compared to, 40–41

UNCLE TOM: as Christ-like martyr, 5–6, 21, 23, 55, 56; death of, 21, 23, 24, 37; Eva's relationship with, 16–18, 19, 20; feminization of, 38–39, 48; as mythic character, 6, 40; Natty Bumpo compared to, 40; and his role in the novel, 10–25, 42, 44; sold to Legree, 18, 24

UNCLE TOM'S CABIN: as abolitionist tract, 36, 38–39; as agent of social change, 28–30; authorial voice in, 8, 22; coincidence in, 21; dramatic power of, 28–30; eruptive force of, 41–43; fairness of, 34–35, 43; God as inspiration for, 42, 47; as Great American Novel, 31; humor in, 32–33, 35, 37; merits of, 39–41; Northern criticism of, 51–52; as a polemic, 5, 43–45; preface to, 10, 42; and Puritan genres, 59–62; racial stereotypes in, 10, 13, 14, 22, 52–53; reader attacked in, 43–45; reception of, 51–53; richness of characterization in, 56; as sentimental novel, 37, 38, 40, 43, 53–54; sources of, 8, 26–28; 33–34, 35–36, 47–48; Southern criticism of, 35–36, 52; stage versions of, 37, 51; structure of, 35, 56, 59–62; success of, 5, 31–33; as Victorian novel, 53–54

WILSON, MR., and his role in the novel, 13–14